Own Your Value

Own Your Value

The Real Future of Pharmacy Practice Revealed

"Try not to become a man of success.

Rather become a man of value." Albert Einstein

By Greg L. Alston PharmD

Copyright Greg L. Alston 2019

Edited by: Julie Sehl

Alchemy Publishing Group
Savannah, GA

ISBN: 978-1-63297-014-5
Paperback Edition
All Rights Reserved
Updated and Republished January 20, 2019

LinkedIn at: https://www.linkedin.com/in/greglalston

DEDICATION

To those who have their heart set on being a good pharmacist and making a good living at the same time but are struggling to make that happen. Now is the time to take control of your own destiny.

ACKNOWLEDGMENTS

We all stand on the shoulders of those who came before us. I learned how to be a professional from my first pharmacy manager Keller. I learned how to be a good manager from the awesome people who let me practice on them at Sav-on Drugs in Inglewood, California. A quick shout out to Shirley Sakamoto and Randy Mello the first pharmacists who had to put up with me. To Carl Vitalie, may he rest in peace, who introduced me to Peter Drucker and the science of management. And finally, to all of you who have worked for me over the years and have made me look good. There are far too many of you to mention all of you by name. But I especially want to mention Shane Desselle and David Zgarrick for letting my join their team on the McGraw-Hill Pharmacy Management text; Tracy Hunter, Jacky Olin and Mike Manolakis for their friendship and guidance; and for the hundreds of students who have put up with me over the years. You have taught me more than I have ever taught you. You have earned my devotion, respect, admiration and undying gratitude.

I would be remiss if I did not acknowledge the following people who have helped mold the man I have become. Thank you to my first love, my high school sweetheart, my prom dates, my first wife, the mother of my children, my best friend, my current wife, my business partner, my current roommate, and the best dispensing pharmacist I have ever met. I can't believe I am lucky enough to have you in my life. It is even more special that you are all the same person. You have put up with me for 49 years so far. Sainthood is in order.

LEGAL DISCLAIMER

This book is presented solely for educational and entertainment purposes. The author and publisher are not offering it as legal, accounting, or other professional services advice. While best efforts have been used in preparing this book, the author and publisher make no representations or warranties of any kind and assume no liabilities of any kind with respect to the accuracy or completeness of the contents and specifically disclaim any implied warranties of merchantability or fitness of use for a particular purpose. Neither the author nor the publisher shall be held liable or responsible to any person or entity with respect to any loss or incidental or consequential damages caused, or alleged to have been caused, directly or indirectly, by the information or programs contained herein. No warranty may be created or extended by sales representatives or written sales materials. Every company and person is different and the advice and strategies contained herein may not be suitable for your situation. You should seek the services of a competent professional before beginning any improvement program. The story and its characters and entities are fictional. Any likeness to actual persons, either living or dead, is strictly coincidental.

Table of Contents

Introduction

The Value Manifesto

If you fail to create value you will fail to thrive. All of life's Rewards flow from creating value for others.

Take the Challenge

Can you convince a potential employer or client that you are worth every penny you are asking for? If you can't explain to someone within 30 seconds why they should pay you what you want, then why would you expect them to pay you at all?

Challenge Part 1: Pull out a 3 x5 index card. When I say go... Write your compelling argument using no more than one side of that card. Assume you have one shot at winning the job. Ready, set, go! Now read your answer aloud. Would it win you the job against all the competitive options out there?

Challenge Part 2: Do you know how to market your value to create and endless stream of income? Can you answer with a confident yes? Can you describe a compelling strategic value advantage that would make your target audience say, " I would be flippin crazy not to hire you!"

Many pharmacists can't sell themselves because they have never learned how. If you want to become value trained to create your own unique pathway to financial freedom then read the rest of this book.

Learn the Change

The career of the American pharmacist is dynamic and ever changing. Hefty sign-on bonuses and multiple job offers are a thing of the past. Global competition, government funded healthcare, and mountains of public debt conspire to create a new reality for the 21st century. Value trained pharmacists recognize this trend and will take steps to secure a bright future for themselves and their families. Will you be one of the pharmacists that change the trajectory of our profession?

Now, Take Charge

Read this manifesto to learn the essential, strategic principles that can insure your financial prosperity, job satisfaction and a rewarding career as a professional pharmacist.

Will you take charge of your own destiny and become valuable?

The Reality of Our Single-minded Viewpoints

After four decades in the pharmacy business in a variety of roles I have worked directly with several thousand community pharmacists, hospital-based pharmacists, academic pharmacists and association based pharmacists. I have been an active participant in executive leadership meetings with independent drug store owners, chain drug executives, drug distribution companies, boards of pharmacy and academic leadership.

I have participated in legislative action at the state and federal level and been actively involved with the APhA, AACP, NCPA, and multiple state associations. I have served on boards, panels, committees, work groups and faculties. And I can tell you that our profession is populated with talented people who practice in a wide variety of roles and functions.

Through all of these experiences one thing has become crystal clear. We are a divided profession. We spend a great deal of time mired in our own points of view and rarely come together to agree on anything. We handicap our profession as a whole because we have a knack for criticizing our differences when we should be celebrating our common bonds. Many of us apparently think that what we do is more important than what "those other" pharmacists do.

Pharmacists seem to enjoy complaining about their lot in life. Interestingly, the complaints most pharmacists have about their working conditions and job opportunities stem from a single root cause: the failure to demonstrate our value.

Historically, the pharmacist's job description has been written by companies that are more attuned to shareholder value than the value pharmacists create for their communities. I have seen this play out in drug chains run by cost cutting productivity managers, in hospitals as hospital pharmacy shifted from profit center to cost center, and even in academia as education standards became more prescriptive and more focused on one definition of a good pharmacist. The mantra has been, "Though Shalt all be Health System Clinicians."

Overall, the drive towards clinical practice is a good thing but the balance of clinical skills with professional business skills needs to be re-examined. There are many ways to use one's education effectively and in order to provide jobs for future generations of pharmacists current pharmacists need to develop new sustainable business models.

Taking off the Blinders

A central committee of planners will not determine the future of the pharmacy profession, the marketplace will. However, the actions **you** take from this day forward will definitely determine your destiny. You can choose to provide valuable goods and services to the marketplace. This will increase the likelihood that you will prosper in your chosen profession. You can also abdicate responsibility for your future to your employer and hope that they act in your best interest. The choice is yours.

I have worked for admirable employers such as Sav-on Drugs, the Jewel Corporation and Smith's Food and Drug only to see them sold to new owners. Sometimes my opportunities were enhanced and sometimes the opposite occurred. Unfortunately, I was never in control of those big decisions. In my experience with large employers when critical decisions are faced, the individual needs of a single employee will always come secondary to the needs of the organization.

What I Believe

For the past 40 years the mantra in many circles of the profession has been that pharmacists who use their pharmacy training to work in community practice pharmacy are wasting a good PharmD degree. Many believe that "clinical" pharmacists only work in healthcare systems settings and that we, as a profession, need to get out of the dispensing business and in to the clinical services business.

But I believe something different. The current mega-trend in the healthcare marketplace is to keep people out of the hospitals as much as possible. Hospitals are financially rewarded for shortening stays and preventing re-admissions. There will always be a need for internal medicine clinical pharmacists in the health system setting. These pharmacists do great work. Yet if they do their jobs well, patients stay out of the hospital. This means that patients will need to receive the longitudinal care they require in a convenient community setting. And those settings already exist. They are called pharmacies and doctor's offices.

If we look at the medication related problems in this country such as drug misadventures, poor adherence, under-diagnosed and untreated conditions, duplicate therapies and generally poor compliance with medication regimens, we as a profession are not doing a very good job for our patients. The National Report on Drug Adherence in America sponsored by NCPA in 2013 rated the profession as a C+ and estimates that poor adherence costs this country $290 billion dollars per year.

My vision of the future is clear. Our highly trained ambulatory care clinicians need to get themselves out of the relatively inaccessible hospital system. They need to embed in community practice locations such as pharmacies and physician's offices to improve patient access to care. No matter how great our internal medicine clinicians are they only have the patients under their care for a few weeks at most. The rest of the year they are back home where they live under the care of a community practice pharmacist.

The future of pharmacy depends upon strengthening the role of community practice. Rather than denigrating community practice, our thought leaders should be encouraging the integration of clinical specialists in operations run by community pharmacy generalists. This would optimize the value of care provided by the profession as a whole.

As a long-time community practice pharmacist, I am mildly offended by the suggestion that what I do is not clinical. No, I do not perform vancomycin dosing. But I am able to detect adverse drug reactions and life threatening medical problems because I know my patients well enough to know when they are not acting right.

Let me give you an example. A regular customer named Maureen was a 68-year-old female of northern European descent with a sunny disposition and a big smile. She usually came by the pharmacy 2-3 times a week and we would always chat. One day she appeared in distress. She was flushed. She had a bad headache. And she stated that she had taken acetaminophen and it didn't help. I sat her down and took her blood pressure. It was 240/200. I immediately had my delivery driver transport her to the emergency room at our hospital and began reviewing her medication profile. The only new medication she had recently begun was a new drug called Vioxx®. I informed the emergency room staff and they stabilized her while discontinuing that drug from her regimen.

As it turns, out this drug was pulled from the market in 2004 because it appeared to cause cardiac events and strokes. At the time of this encounter, however, none of this information was in the literature and the only reason this lady did not suffer a life threatening event was because I knew her well enough to know she wasn't acting right.

This does not happen every day in any one pharmacy, but it does happen every day in a pharmacy somewhere in our country. And more importantly this is most certainly "clinical" pharmacy.

Does the typical employed pharmacist have the time to know his/her customers well? Do they observe everything they should observe? And do they respond appropriately when they detect a problem? Not if they are overworked and understaffed. In my experience, a well run independent drug store is more likely to provide this high level of service that an understaffed chain store, but that is just my opinion.

Look at this logically. We need to re-envision the practice of pharmacy. We need to describe the community practice pharmacist as the primary care generalist. We need to use our residency-trained clinicians to provide specialty care in a community based location. I will talk more about this later. Our schools and board exams focus on acute care institutional medicine when the vast majority of total patient interactions occur in continuity of care, community environments.

To all the pessimists out there

There are a great number of pharmacists who appear to be miserable and angry all the time. They complain Online, they complain at work and they complain that they don't have enough time to complain. Many of those folks will read what I have to say and scoff. They will accuse me of not knowing anything about how screwed up the pharmacy profession has become. But here is the truth as I see it.

Whining is for losers. If you want to associate yourself with losers, then do so. Put this book down and go be a loser. I see some of the crummy stuff going on in the field and choose to think it can be done better. I believe individual, energetic and optimistic pharmacists armed with the right professional business skills can excel as providers of value to those they serve.

If you want to be part of the problem then go hang out with the whiners. But if you want to be part of the solution then read the rest of what I have to say. All the problems we face are solvable and they will not be solved by whining but by innovative action that brings the disparate voices in this profession to bear on solving the health care needs of our citizens.

PERSONAL DISCLAIMER

I have been active in the profession since 1975 and have heard all the rhetoric for years as we went from being pharmacists, to clinical pharmacists, to pharmaceutical care providers, to Medication Therapy Management, to Primary Care pharmacists. The reality is that the constant reinventing of the label we used to identify our profession has had no positive impact on the marketplace. The reality is that good pharmacists solve problems for their patients and/or clients and always have regardless of what we call it.

The attempt to define ourselves using the terminology du-jour has not done anything to move the profession forward. Along the way we have allowed non pharmacists to define our value. Our profession has a lot to offer so I ask that your read this book in the spirit in which it was intended.

I want each of you to excel at what you do and provide value to your stakeholders while creating financial security for your families.

The opinions expressed in this book belong solely to the author and are meant to be provocative. They are not intended to be demeaning or degrading to any one person, organization, or company. My sole intent is to challenge the members of this profession to stop fighting amongst themselves and start creating value in the marketplace. I happen to believe many of the prevailing axioms being reflexively repeated by many "leaders" in the profession are not true.

Axiom 1

The first axiom I believe is misguided is the 'Field of Dreams' strategy. In the 1989 movie of this name an Iowa farmer played by Kevin Costner hears a voice in his cornfield that tells him, "If you build it, he will come" He builds a baseball field on his farm and as a result reunites with his father and his past.

Many within our profession espouse the axiom that if we develop better clinical skills the world will magically demand to pay us for these skills. But this 'dream' has not paid off as well as the movie version. Over the past 40 years, we have greatly improved the clinical skills of our graduates and nevertheless, are still fighting to get paid as providers of services.

This does not mean that developing these skills was wrong, but it does mean that we have done a miserable job of marketing these skills effectively. When our residency-trained clinical specialists in the health system setting are being paid less than an entry level generalist in community practice, it is hard to argue that we have sold the value of pharmacist clinical skills well.

Axiom 2

The second axiom that has been repeated for years, is that our profession should get out of the dispensing business and in to the clinical services business. The unintended consequence of this belief has been that a lot of graduates of PharmD programs have focused their training on development of their clinical skills to the exclusion of their professional business skills. The absence of these skills is precisely why they are unable to communicate their value effectively to get paid what they are worth. And I think that some of the people pushing this logic need to reflect on the reality of our free market economy.

If we fail to provide value and market it effectively, we will not get paid what we are worth. If we give up our control of the dispensing function we will have no guaranteed access to patients. Without patients, we will not get paid at all.

The solution is not to jettison our clinical training but to enhance our business training. The ultimate question is how that training can possibly fit in to a curriculum that is stocked full of basic science, therapeutics, kinetics, calculations, inter-professional education, experiential rotations and preparation for a board exam largely based on acute care therapeutics.

Axiom 3

The third frequently repeated axiom that I believe is provable false is that technology will free the pharmacist to provide more clinical services. Many people misunderstand the difference between 'sustaining innovation' and 'disruptive innovation'. A sustaining innovation helps an existing business model be more efficient and more profitable. Advanced computerized dispensing devices, robotics, central-fill and increased use of technicians are sustaining innovations that improve the profitability of their companies by eliminating the need for highly paid pharmacist help. They actually decrease the number of pharmacists needed to get the prescriptions dispensed. For many in the chain drug and hospital sectors technology has cost jobs and led to a more process driven role than a clinical role for those who remain employed.

Disruptive innovations are those innovations that create new business models and expand opportunities. Innovations like Amazon and Uber have clearly disrupted traditional business models. Mall stores have trouble competing now as do taxi cabs. There are technologies available now that could drastically disrupt the market and expand the need for personalized healthcare service provided by pharmacists. But if our thought leaders continue to use these terms as if they were interchangeable it is unlikely they will drive the change necessary to enable these new types of business models. Not all technology or innovation has the effect of improving healthcare outcomes. Many just improve corporate profit.

The key to developing pharmacist-created disruptive innovation is to teach them the value creation skills they need to expand patient services and disrupt the old way of delivering healthcare. Patients don't need endless policy discussions they need innovative solutions to their most pressing needs. Pharmacists need to become value-trained to learn how to build these disruptive innovations.

Is this something students can comprehend and have time for during their classroom training? Is it best left to be taught after they leave the classroom? Does every student need this training or just those who show an aptitude for it? Can 10-15% of the graduating class build enough new business models to be able to hire the rest of their classmates?

These are great questions and I invite the debate to begin. All I know for sure is that our profession holds a unique place in the culture of our nation and we will lose that place if we don't change some of our own self-defeating strategies.

CHAPTER 1

Become a VIP

I advocate that pharmacists working in any type of setting take responsibility for their individual success by becoming a "Valuable Innovative Pharmacist"(VIP). What does this mean? It means becoming someone who is in control of their own value.

The classic method of controlling your own destiny in community practice has been to operate your own drug store. Given the consolidation in the chain drug industry, and the development of new sources of lending, this is still one of the best ways to take charge of your own career and prosper. Unfortunately, you can't just buy a business and expect it to be successful. You must learn the right way to own, and operate, a 21st century pharmacy business if you hope to thrive. More importantly, there are many more potential pharmacy businesses than just a traditional drug store. Indeed, there are a variety of ways to gain more control of your career without owning your own business at all.

Identifying Value Sources

Imagine that you could become a VIP pharmacist without having to quit your current job. Would that reduce your fear of getting started? For example, a valuable pharmacist could develop a new patient service for her existing employer that adds value to her role in the company.

A VIP could modify or improve company processes that illustrate her enhanced value to an organization and reduce the likelihood of being eliminated in a downsizing.

A VIP could master a new skill that the organization needs to have performed.

A VIP could develop an entirely new business model that allows her to practice where, when and how she wants to practice.

In any event, a Valuable Innovative Pharmacist will be the kind of person who will be sought for her expertise, rewarded for her performance and always be able to generate the income needed to provide for her family's wants and needs.

Quotable Thought

A VIP recognizes and acts upon opportunities and leverages her skills to create value for others

Try to keep an open mind and entertain new possibilities. In the highly competitive global economy, the future will belong to people who do one of two things, They will:

1. Become a VIP, or,

2. Work with someone who is.

Mediocre pharmacists may have trouble finding good jobs. If you are <u>not</u> trying to be the best in the world at what you do then by default, you are endeavoring to be mediocre. Mediocre pharmacists won't thrive.

Nothing Stays The Same... Will You?

Since 1975, when I began as a pharmacy intern, the world of pharmacy has changed dramatically. Counseling patients was not allowed, because physicians didn't want us scaring their patients by discussing drug side effects. Now pharmacists work shoulder to shoulder with physicians in non-traditional roles and are required to counsel. We have gone from a bachelor's degree, with an elective course in therapeutics, to a clinical doctorate degree as the entry level degree. Our dispensing business has evolved from getting paid in cash at a 45% gross margin, to loaning hundreds of thousands of dollars to Pharmacy Benefit Managers (PBMs) at 18% gross margin. And, we have gone from no prescription coverage for the typical family to the federal government as a primary payer.

I don't have a crystal ball to predict the future. Nevertheless, I think it is a safe bet to believe that the future will be vastly different than the present. I think it is safe to assume that, 1) the gross margin on dispensing prescriptions is not heading higher any time soon, 2) there will be more government regulation and not less, and 3) that the amortization of our enormous public debt will eventually drive public policy regarding health care spending.

Therefore, I think it is safe to assume that the only way pharmacists will thrive in the future is by developing skills that allow them to perform their jobs at a high performance level. The essential question that you must answer is, "What are you going to be able to do to earn the compensation you want?"

I worked most of my professional practice life in community practice pharmacy, both as a chain drug employee and an independent owner. However, I believe that a good value strategy is applicable to any professional practice role. Most of the examples I will use in this book will be community pharmacist based. First, because that is what I know best, and second, because I can draw on a rich supply of stories from that practice setting. But I will also share with you some awesome examples of pharmacist entrepreneurs who are already creating new and exciting business models in novel practice settings. Try to avoid fixating on the example; rather look to the example as an illustration of how the principles of what I am talking about can be applied. This manifesto...which by definition means a declaration of principles...will hopefully take you on the journey to discovering your own unique answers to insuring a rewarding and profitable future. During this process I hope you will become a Valuable Innovative Pharmacist.

If you are not practicing at the top of your profession then what are you going to do to change? You can't continue to do things the way you have always done them and hope to see any improvement. To succeed in the future you will have to develop your value creation skills. In order to grow you will have to change. The two key issues are: 1) what change is needed? And 2) how do you learn this change?

First and foremost, you need to do something different from everybody else if you expect to get different results than everybody else. If you want to create a bulletproof career, (a career in which you will always be employed), you must offer more value than the average pharmacist.

You can learn to offer that value by studying, 1) how value is created, 2) how to market that value to others and, 3) how to sustain that value over time by continuing to innovate. See the last section of this book, resources for you, to gain access to a free video series that explains the basics of these three concepts.

The Curtain Rises

The Three-Act plot structure is a model used in classic story telling. It divides a story into three parts called the Setup, the Confrontation and the Resolution. Each act serves a purpose.

In the first act, the author lays the groundwork by introducing the characters and describing the world they live in. The job of the first act is to put the character in context for the reader and describe the first turning point in the story.

The second act typically depicts the protagonist's attempt to resolve a major problem in her life, only to find herself in ever -worsening situations. She usually is unable to resolve this problem because she lacks the skills to deal with the forces of antagonism. The protagonist must not only learn new skills, but also develop a better sense of whom she is and what she is capable of, in order to deal with her predicament.

In short, she must change in order to win. In a good story, the hero is usually aided by a mentor who helps her reach her goals. At the end of act two, the protagonist is usually in danger and the audience (or readers) fears for her safety.

Act three describes the resolution. In the resolution phase of the story, the protagonist will overcome her tragic flaws. These character flaws have prevented the hero from having success in the past, but in the third act she overcomes those flaws and raises up to defeat the threat. This may occur by suddenly recognizing opportunities and leveraging them to success. The audience will be relieved and applaud because they want the hero to win.

The story of the practice of pharmacy is being written. Acts one and two have been recorded. What will you do to make sure that act three goes the way you hope it will go?

CHAPTER 2

The Story

In my proposed act one, I will introduce you to Gina, our local pharmacist hero. She is a leader in the community, hires her neighbors to work for her, pays local taxes, is a member of the local Chamber of Commerce, serves on local community boards, and is a well-respected person. Gina provides personalized attention and care to every person she serves.

In act two Gina is under relentless attack. The big-box chain stores have opened up on every corner, the evil middlemen have driven her customers into mail-order, pharmacy reimbursement strategies have strangled her cash flow, burdensome regulations have raised her costs of operations, and Gina is tired, worn out, discouraged, and feeling unappreciated. Available job opportunities are diminishing and are not that exciting.

But then a transformation occurs in act three. A light bulb goes on! Our discouraged shopkeeper becomes the champion of individualized patient care. Gina bravely fights the regulatory battles, circumvents the middlemen, and creates true value for her customers.

She cleverly learns to diversify the dispensing operation into a variety of additional services. Gina no longer relies 100% on prescription volume as a profit driver and she develops additional skills, identifies unique market niches, and learns to capitalize on those niches by taking advantage of new technology to win the marketing battle for the hearts and minds of patients.

She learns to partner with other pharmacists to offer fee-based services that she does not have the expertise to perform herself. She leverages the expertise of a coalition of pharmacists who offer specialized care in hormone replacement, diabetic education, AIDS services, genomic testing, weight loss, asthma management, anti-coagulation clinics, hospice care, assisted living services, specialty drug care, medication therapy management services, Medicare Part D services, elder care, fibromyalgia care, stress management, autism services, proper nutrition, naturopathic care, specialty compounding services, immunization services, and a host of other individualized patient care services.

Quotable Thought

The unique relationship of trust between pharmacist and patient is the foundation for innovation

And finally, as a result of her professional partnerships, she becomes revered in the local community and is beloved by all. This version of act three is possible for anyone but only by adding business skills to your personal skill set to create a value strategy that is right for your skill set.

The biggest untapped resource available to move the profession of pharmacy forward is the data locked within the pharmacy dispensing computers in every pharmacy in America. If you had the professional referral relationship network built with the breadth of specialty practitioners I mentioned above, how hard would it be to identify the patients that needed those services?

What if there was a networked system that allowed you to identify, hire, pay and rate clinical consultants to treat your patients?

What if you had a patient medical record system that let everyone know the progress of the patient? Wouldn't that be amazing?

A Look at Bench-to-Business History

The origins of the profession are rooted in community-based commerce, originating hundreds of years ago, where the first pharmacists were essentially shopkeepers mixing and selling potions directly to customers. There was no formal training or schools of pharmacy; a young person was simply apprenticed to a pharmacist and learned their craft on the job.

Then, in the early 1900's, this began to change as growth during the industrial revolution saw the founding of companies that manufactured medications to sell. These manufacturing companies created pills, capsules and elixirs to treat various maladies. A variety of medications were packaged and often sold with little regard for whether they actually worked or contained harmful ingredients.

Becoming A Trusted Authority

As the pharmacist transitioned from the maker of all medicines to the seller of all medicines, he added value to the ingredients by offering to share his knowledge of how to use those medicines properly. Eventually pharmacist training became standardized and required pharmacists to become licensed. This was done in order to protect the public from unscientific pharmaceutical practices and unsafe medicines that were being sold.

As independent store owners flourished, some of them began to open multiple locations. Thus began the chain drug industry. The drug chains that survive today were spawned as independent businesses. This interconnection between pharmacy and business has existed from the beginning.

Whereas physicians and nurses also provided patient care, the unique relationship between the pharmacist and the community thrived precisely because of the duality of roles that the pharmacist played by interacting with the both patient and the doctors who treated them.

Pharmacists became the gateway to the health care system and serve as the primary care triage centers for the health care system in the United States. The mental image generated by the word "pharmacist" in the minds of the American consumer is that of a person who dispenses medications from a community pharmacy.

Pharmacist entrepreneurs have a long, and fascinating history of innovation. Dr. Pepper, Pepsi-Cola and Coca-Cola were invented in a pharmacy. The first drug chains, the first 24-hour store, the first drive-through window, the first food and drug combination store, the first office practice, the first disease management services, and the first immunization practices were developed by individual pharmacists. Unburdened by the layers of management required to generate a corporate decision, free-thinking individual pharmacists continue to innovate and introduce new products and services ahead of any industry timetable.

As new practice opportunities have arisen, the training of pharmacists has improved. Less than 35 years ago, therapeutics was barely taught at most schools of pharmacy. However, with the mandate of the Doctor of Pharmacy degree as the entry-level pharmacy credential, the nature of pharmacy education underwent a metamorphosis. And so did the expectations placed on a pharmacy school graduate. With the new ACPE educational standards of 2016 schools must not only cover the traditional science and therapeutics but now must integrate what used to be called extracurricular and co-curricular activities in to the program as well.

Crossing Swords: Academia Versus Real-Life Practice

With the drive towards primary care clinical pharmacists fully underway, the schools of pharmacy added clinical rotations and advanced therapeutic coursework prompting an unpleasant schism to develop between community practice and academia. As academia attempted to prepare students for the pharmacy of the future, the actual practice of pharmacy had stubbornly refused to change at the same pace. And despite the academic clamor for clinical practice there has been little concomitant demand from the public to pay for such services. Therefore, tension developed between the community practitioners trying to operate the businesses of pharmacy, and pharmacy school graduates who had no interest in running a business. These graduates wanted to practice clinical pharmacy not lowly "retail" pharmacy.

Regrettably, This Tension is Not Fully Resolved

As a practicing community pharmacist, I often wondered whether academics had any clue about how "real" pharmacists worked. Of course, I was prey to my own biased viewpoint. After joining academia, I was pleasantly surprised to find out that most of my assumptions about academic pharmacists were wrong. What I perceived as animosity towards community practice was not driven by any underlying dislike for community practice, but was driven by a more subtle driver. Most of the clinical faculty I have met are incredibly talented at what they do. But what they do is not traditional community practice. And for many, their only real exposure to community practice pharmacy had been the chain drug practice of pharmacy. Chain practice is only one version of community practice. And in my clearly biased opinion, it is not necessarily the highest form. Let me explain this comment further.

Examining Chain Versus Independent Pharmacies

I want to spend a few minutes comparing chain drug and independently owned pharmacies to provide an example of how there are many different ways to craft a value strategy. Chain drug is one way to practice but it is a different way than independent ownership. I will attempt to illustrate this example by positing how an independent pharmacist can become more valuable than a large, corporate pharmacy operation for the community it serves.

While chain drug pharmacy and independent pharmacy may appear to be the same, there are significant differences between the two. I feel uniquely qualified to comment on these differences because I have lived and managed in both worlds. I devoted 15 years of my life to chain drug management in a variety of corporate level positions: for three different drug chains including, Sav-on Drugs, Thrifty Drug Stores and Smith's Food and Drug. In addition, I was the owner/operator of high volume independent drug stores for another 15 years. Here is what I see as the essential difference between the two.

A chain drug operator must rely on systems, policies and procedures to produce a similar result in all of their locations. It is very difficult for chains to succeed without a reproducible business system. While systems allow them to scale and grow their business it also presents many challenges.

It is very difficult to reward stellar performers and just as difficult to penalize under performers. No matter how you slice it, at the end of the day a percentage of the workforce is worth a lot more than they are paid, and a percentage of the workforce is not worth what they're paid. When the chain faces challenges, it is difficult to innovate and roll out a solution that will work in all locations.

Because ultimately, the execution of the plan depends on the engagement of the local pharmacist. Unfortunately, when money gets tight and pressure is on earnings, the most rapid and effective way to increase corporate earnings is to decrease payroll. This irritates the staff and produces the exact opposite of an engaged employee.

Quotable Thought

The independent pharmacy practice is fundamentally different from the chain drug practice environment.

Once a business goes through a cycle of decreased payroll it becomes very difficult to re-engage sales growth. Much of the sales growth for modern chain drugstore companies currently comes from the addition of new stores and not from incremental year-over-year sales growth of the individual stores. The end result is that employees can end up with a feeling that they are being asked to do more and more with less and less.

In the good old days when there were multiple chains and multiple employment options, it was easy for a good chain drug pharmacist to change jobs and switch companies. With industry consolidation and only a few players left standing, the opportunity is greatly diminished to switch from chain to chain. If you have already worked for the big three and not enjoyed that experience, what do you do next? One option is to go from chain to independent. Smart independent owners can easily hire away good chain pharmacists by offering them a different work experience.

It is a fact of life that people join good companies but quit bad managers. All it takes is for one bad manager to spend enough time aggravating employees to cause them to leave a company and go to work for somebody else. This is a very difficult problem for a multi-state chain drug operator to control. Even if an employee likes the company, an individual bad manager can chase them off.

Therefore, while chain drugstores and independent drugstores both operate retail locations and both fill prescriptions as their primary source of revenue, this is about where the similarity ends. While any well-run pharmacy must have good business systems in order to consistently remain profitable, independent pharmacists can much more easily tailor those systems to meet the needs of the local population.

The Payoff And Perils Of Independents

For example, if an independent store is located in a predominantly senior citizen neighborhood they could add additional front-end help to walk the aisles and actually help the older customer shop. They could add additional registers, because the older person takes longer to write a check than a young person takes to swipe an ATM card. Many seniors have difficulty walking, so they could cut down the distance from the front of the store to the pharmacy to minimize that walk. And they could offer home delivery for those instances when an older person can't get to the store on their own.

Just like their chain counterparts, independent store owners also have to worry about developing pay and incentive packages for their employees. But they have the increased flexibility to customize a package to fit the needs of an individual. It is very common to find special accommodations made for employees in an independent setting. And since the independent owner has total control over the hours of operation and the days worked, this flexibility extends beyond wage rates and workdays to any element of the employment experience including the scheduling flexibility to deal with the demands of child care.

Let Me Give You One Example

When my wife and I ran our store in Sun City, California we were open from 8:30 – 5:30 Monday through Friday and 9:00 to 1:00 on Saturday. We filled 1000 prescriptions on a Monday and averaged about 600 per day every other weekday and about 200 on Saturday. It was a busy shop. We were closed every Sunday and holiday. One of the biggest complaints chain pharmacists have is that they get stuck working nights, weekends, and holidays for 40 years. We had no problem hiring the best people because we had better working conditions and better hours. The only reason chain stores are open those crazy long hours is because they are. They do not need to be. They are simply afraid not to be.

By staying open these long hours the typical two pharmacist shift only overlaps for a few hours per day between lunch and dinner. Essentially there is only one pharmacist on duty for the majority of the day. If you get stuck on one problem you are behind all day long. By compressing a two pharmacist shift in to a 9-hour day you have overlap all day long except for the lunch breaks. The result is much better customer service and a greater capacity to deal with problems effectively. It actually encourages your team to solve problems rather than avoid them.

But hours and working conditions are not the most significant difference between the chain drug and independent store operations. Ultimately, the fundamental difference is that the independent owner almost always attacks an earnings problem with an entirely different strategy than the chain drug executive. Whereas chain drug operators typically cut payroll to improve earnings, an independent operator is reluctant to cut payroll. Their first option is to seek out new sales.

The drive for new sales fuels the innovation that is evident in a well-run independent pharmacy. There are only two options for improving earnings in a world where gross margins are largely controlled by third parties. A pharmacy must either, 1) increase sales (and by default improve gross margin dollars) or 2) cut expenses. Since the single largest controllable expense for any retail operation is typically payroll, that is why chain-store operators cut payroll when earnings are lean.

An independent owner feels an obligation to her employees. She knows them well and knows their families. Employees need every penny they can muster to fuel their family budgets. Owners are very reluctant to look a colleague in the eye and say, "I need to cut your pay or your hours." Although this does happen sometimes, it is not the first course of action that independents prefer to take. They would much rather creates incentives for the staff to produce new sales and growth to fund company earnings. This may not sound earth shattering to someone who has not owned and operated a pharmacy. The reality is that these two different approaches set the tone for an organization. And it is this tone that drives employee engagement.

Oh, and by the way, our pharmacy had a Walgreen's, Rite-Aid and a Von's Grocery store pharmacy right in our parking lot. In addition, there were two other independent stores in the same town of only 15,000 people. And we filled more prescriptions than all of them combined. If you know how to run your business correctly you can obliterate any competitor. Assuming you have access to the patients and are not locked out by the PBM.

Let me pose this question a different way to independent store owners who are looking for ways to grow their profits. What if you could sub-contract advanced patient care to other specialty pharmacist partners and generate new profitable revenue as a result? Could you improve your profits with new sales that had no associated cost of goods?

Why does this matter to you if you don't want to be an independent store owner?

You should care about what happens to independent pharmacies in this country for several reasons. Some are in the best interest of the profession and some are purely selfish. First the professional business skills you need to be successful in your career are the very same skills necessary to carve out your own retail business. Therefore, learning these skills and listening to these examples will help you whether you choose to be an entrepreneur or an intrapreneur.

Essentially, you must learn what makes you unique and develop your value strategy to attract income. Additionally, companies that value their employees and build a strong customer focused business are much more engaging places to work. It is truly unfortunate that as the number of drug chains has diminished the work environment for many pharmacists seems to have degraded as well. As companies grows larger they seem to gravitate toward an industrial control model that devalues the individual decision making capacity of the local pharmacist. In my opinion this has hurt the ability of the local pharmacist to provide the patient care needed to improve individual patient outcomes.

If you need to look for a job you may want to consider working for an independent store owner. There are good ones and bad ones just like any industry. However, the experience is entirely different than working in a chain drug environment.

And once again it is my opinion that real disruptive innovation will always occur in an entrepreneurial environment, and that you are more likely to find that environment in an independently owned business.

In addition, if you want to start any type of patient care service, you will need to have access to patients. One of the most viable ways to access patients will be to partner with independent pharmacies.

I will share some resources at the end of this book that can help you develop these skills. In my opinion your pharmacy degree will get you a job but your business skills will be what makes you wealthy. And I use the term wealthy to include all forms of remuneration not just financial. Each person has their own balance of income, freedom, flexibility and fame that they are looking to achieve. Paradoxically, it is your ability to create value for authors that will create the value in your life as well.

Quotable Thought

A company that emphasizes profitability will never win the hearts of its customers. A company that focuses on creating transformational value for its customers will be rewarded with profits.

CHAPTER 3
Get Engaged

The Gallup organization has done stellar work in identifying the keys to success for a customer service-based organization. They published this work in a book called the *Human Sigma: Managing the Employee-Customer Encounter* (John Fleming Gallup Press 2007). If you want to provide a successful pharmacy service, you should read this book.

The biggest take-away point from the book is that the fundamental difference between a successful and unsuccessful service-based organization is the level of engagement of its employees and its customers. Engaged employees and customers are active advocates for the success of the business. Disengaged employees actively undermine the success of their business. The key to the success of independent pharmacy has been the tremendous engagement of its employees in the mission and values of independent practice.

Successful independent pharmacies are driven by a commitment to patient care. They reflect this commitment in the way they treat their employees, the way they treat their customers, and their engagement in the community. This is why strong community independent pharmacy stores continue to outperform individual chain drug locations in many cases. And this opens the way for independent store owners to partner with pharmacist entrepreneurs to expand the kinds of services that can add value for their patients and generate revenue for both.

If you have worked for a good independent owner-operator, then you know what I'm talking about. If you have not, then

I encourage you to go meet one. If you don't know where to meet one, then I suggest you contact pharmacist Dan Benamoz's team at Pharmacy Development Service (PDS) in Florida. I have been to his conference several times and it is the most exciting three-day event I have ever been to.

Your head will explode with the incredible entrepreneurial energy you will experience at the annual February event. And you will meet the most amazing bunch of pharmacy owners and business minded thought leaders in the profession. This is not a wholesaler conference, this is a mind expanding entrepreneur fest. If you want to understand the possibilities of community pharmacy practice then go and stay for the full three days. You will never be the same. I will provide the contact information at the end of this book.

But back to the chain versus independent story. I still have many friends in upper management at some of the big chain drug companies. There is a conversation I had with one that I want to share with you. I had the opportunity to meet with the vice-president of operations for one of the large drug chains and have him visit my store in Sun City, California. We had a great conversation and shared dinner together that evening.

He said one thing to me that I believe makes my point. Now understand that he was the operations manager for about 600 well respected chain drug outlets at that time. And we had known each other for 25 years. But what he said to me was this: "I love coming in to your store. There's just an entirely different vibe than we have in our stores."

The subtext of this compliment is crucial. A chain can copy the independent's floor plan, layout and work-flow system but it can't duplicate the energy and enthusiasm created by a community of "engaged" employees serving engaged customers. Imagine how powerful a drug chain would be if it could capture this energy in all of their stores! But big bureaucracies have a lot of trouble figuring out how to do that.

And again, my point is not to convince you to buy your own drug store. But I want to challenge you to take charge of your own value and make decisions based on truth not rumor. Local pharmacies continue to thrive because they offer a valuable experience to local residents that chain stores do not. Chains do what they do. Independents do what they do. They serve different needs and different customers.

Valuable Innovative Pharmacists will thrive for the same reason. They have carved out a niche and do it better than anyone else. If you don't want to be a store owner can you develop a professional expertise that would allow you to partner with a store owner to provide new clinical services to her patients? Can the store owner play the role of generalist who identifies patient needs and then subcontracts with the best pharmacist to meet those needs? Can the pharmacists who have developed a niche business model then play the role of the specialist to provide high quality targeted care?

Let me give you a few examples of some niches that entrepreneurial pharmacists have developed in to successful businesses.

The first one I will share with you is **Dr. Anna Garrett**. Anna has built a niche practice centered on helping women in midlife who are struggling with managing Peri-menopause or menopause symptoms. She helps them find non-pharmaceutical alternatives to get their hormones in balance so they can live happy healthy lives. She also co-founded the Medipreneurs.

Matt Johnson is a pharmacist and co-founder of Amplicare, a software company with the mission to create tools that help turn pharmacists into healthcare superheroes. His I-Medicare iPad app now has over 5,000 subscribers and helps store owners maximize patient Medicare Part D choices.

Jeff Jellin is a fraternity brother from the University of the Pacific, who helped launch a newsletter about 40 years ago that has become one of the premier publications in the profession, called *The Pharmacist's Letter*, with hundreds of thousands of prescribers.

Dan Benamoz of Pharmacy Development Service has created a phenomenal organization that helps store owners improve what they do and how much they make doing it. His organization is growing in both size and impact every year.

Blair Thielemier, PharmD, has developed a pharmacist consultant company to teach pharmacists how to partner with physician's offices to provide full blown MTM services. She also developed the Pharmapreneur Academy and the Elevate Pharmacy Summit and is now pushing in to Genetic testing.

Michelle Fritsch, PharmD, founded Meds Mash to provide medication management and coaching for senior citizens to maximize their quality of life. She also co-founded Medipreneurs.

Sue Paul, RPh, is the president and founder of SyneRxgy Consulting. She helps people by helping physicians create accurate lists of the medications people are actually on and has added genomic testing to her repertoire. She has her own take on targeted MTM services for patients and also co-founded Medipreneurs. And by the way, she has been too busy to get a PharmD, but not too busy to create value for her patients.

And **Patti Manolakis** hasn't practiced in a traditional pharmacy practice for the last 20 years. I got to know Patti because her husband Michael and I worked together for many years at Wingate University. Patti has run her own consulting practice (PMM Consulting) for years and has done brilliant work for many organizations like APhA and the Board of Pharmacy Specialties.

She has become a nationally recognized expert in her field who has had a significant impact on a wide range of public policy issues including the removal of unsafe pediatric formulations from the market and the documentation of new pharmacy specialties for certification. She was way ahead of her time in learning to carve out a niche practice she could run from home while raising three boys and a husband.

There are some amazing pharmacists out there doing awesome things. And the key to their success is that they did not sit around waiting for somebody's permission to take action. They found a need and created a service to meet that need. They didn't wait to become an official provider they just started providing.

Your success will be 100% dependent upon your ability to find a problem that needs solving and figuring out how to get paid to solve that problem. By focusing on solving other people's problems income will flow to you. If you fixate on making money you will find that people will avoid you whenever they can.

Engagement Is The Barometer Of Success

Customer satisfaction surveys really miss the point. The question is not "Did we meet all your needs when you came into the store today?" People can be very satisfied with what they got, but not be enthusiastic about it.

To use a retail example, customers do not shop exclusively in one location. A customer might stop in one store on Thursday because it's near where she gets her nails done. Or she may drop in there to buy a soda. She might shop at another store on Saturday because it's next door to the grocery store. And she might shop at another store on Monday because it's on the way home from work. There is a big difference between a shopping trip of convenience and someone who will go out of their way and pass up competitors to come to you.

Engaged customers are not just satisfied with the service, they love the service and they tell all of their friends. They shop with you because of you. The competitive advantage that an independent (either drug store or niche specialty) pharmacy business has is the personality and demeanor of the pharmacist.

Quotable Thought

Engaged Customers shop with you because they love the service and trust your expertise!

Learn to think independently. Far too many pharmacists don't understand the amazing opportunity that is directly in front of them. They only see what is and not what could be. They look at the state of the job market and see pessimism and doom and gloom.

I look at the state of the marketplace and see an incredible number of huge problems. For the pharmacist untrained in value theory, a problem is an obstacle to success. For the value trained, a problem is a opportunity to create a new niche business. There has never been more opportunity than there is today. But you have to learn how to see it and capitalize on it.

The big problems will keep the mediocre pharmacist from trying to solve them, which creates an incredibly powerful strategic advantage for a value trained independent thinker. Let us revisit what it is like to be a pharmacist in today's marketplace.

For many years, the chain drug industry was growing steadily and many pharmacists were hired, not because they were particularly great pharmacists, but because they were needed to open up the store. While that allowed the chain to expand, it likely diluted their ability to compete on service. Now that the employment market has tightened up, many of these non-engaged employees are being traded out for new graduates. This process of getting rid of long-term marginal employees in favor of lower cost new graduates helps reduce payroll. However, it severely damages the engagement level of the remaining employees. They are left wondering how they will be treated when they get their 10-year pins.

When I was a regional pharmacy supervisor for Thrifty Drugs and the California supervisor for Smith's Food and Drugs, I had the opportunity to manage over 150 stores for those chains. Some locations are naturally better than others. But even in the chain environment, if I put a mediocre pharmacist in a good store the prescription volume would go down. If I put a great pharmacist in the same store the prescription volume would go up.

Of course, there were limits to what you could do with no traffic in the store, but in every single case the pharmacists that went out of their way to serve the public improved the sales of the store.

To those of you not yet value trained, please understand the point I am trying to make. The quality of the pharmacist makes a huge difference in the quality of the service provided. The quality of the service provided determines the engagement level of the customers.

The engagement level of the customers determines the profitability of the business.

If you allow your value to be determined by corporate bean counters or bureaucrats, then don't be surprised if you are unhappy with their determination of your value. If you want to control the amount of money you make, the amount of free time you have and the amount of freedom you have to practice your profession the way you want to practice, then you have to learn how to control your own value strategy.

A good independent pharmacy owner knows the value of a high quality pharmacist. And these owners are much more invested in the outcome of their individual locations than a chain supervisor is for any one location. Therefore, in the local market, a good strong independent drugstore will frequently outperform the average chain store outlet. Caveat: as long as they have access to the customers and are not shut out of the networks. (I will deal with this later in this book.)

Therefore, if we had an army of independent pharmacy contractors who specialized in solving real problems for their stakeholders then we could redefine what it means to be a pharmacist. And we could do it on our own terms. We could partner store owners with access to patients with specialists who could provide advanced services. We do not have to limit ourselves to what large corporate employers or Pharmacy Benefit Managers think we are.

If this is something you are interested in then engage in the conversation wherever and whenever you can. The greatest hurdle to your becoming a VIP are your own self-imposed limits.

CHAPTER 4
Recognize The Challenge

Today's retail pharmacy has come under relentless attack by the forces at play in the healthcare marketplace. Retail gross margins on prescriptions in 1985 were approximately 45% of sales. Retail gross margins on brand-name drugs today are less than 10%. You might think that this margin reduction has been driven by competition or by the economic times. But it has not. It is the result of forces from a unique set of middlemen that have carved out a niche in the center of the drug distribution and dispensing chain.

Most retail industries started out in a multi-tiered structure. The producer would sell to a wholesaler, the wholesaler would sell to a retailer, and the retailer would sell to the consumer. In the drug product distribution arm of the retail drug industry this is how a product moves from the drug manufacturer to the drug wholesaler to the drugstore to the consumer.

Unlike most free-market industries, the pharmacy payment systems for the purchases have become divorced from the product distribution system. It was not until the 1980s when third-party payment for prescription drugs really began in earnest. And it was not until the mid-1980s that drug stores began computerizing their pharmacies. With the advent of computerized prescription records the development of prescription drug data management began. This data management process then evolved into a network development process. And finally, it morphed in to a complex, unregulated, extremely profitable, self-serving, business model of pharmacy benefit management.

Essentially what occurred is that a relatively streamlined product distribution system has been counterbalanced by a relatively convoluted payment system. In the old "cash transaction model," a drug manufacturer sold their product to the wholesaler, who sold their product to the pharmacy, who sold their product to the consumer. This was simple and straightforward.

In the pharmacy third-party payment model, the controller of the patient--the HMO or insurance company-- contracts with the benefit management firm (called the Pharmacy Benefit Manager--PBM) to set up a network of pharmacy providers. The pharmacy providers are layered into tiers, based on the lowest level of reimbursement they will accept. The customer is told which pharmacy provider to go to, and the payment structure is designed to drive patient to mail order pharmacies owned by the PBM.

The benefit manager company collects money from the payer (i.e. the employer) to provide for about 80% of the cost of the prescription. The customer pays only about 20% of the cost of the prescription at the counter in the pharmacy. Once the pharmacist dispenses the medication he collects that 20% from the patient and sends a bill to the pharmacy benefit manager for the remaining 80%. Somewhere between 20 and 45 days later the pharmacy gets a check for the 80%. Not straightforward, never simple. Obviously, this convoluted pathway presents quite a few problems.

How This Impacts Profitability

When the pharmacy has to pay 100% of the wholesale price for the drug, but only collects 20% of the retail price in cash from the customer prior to paying this bill, this creates cash flow problems. For example, if the benefit manager delays payment, the pharmacy must fund the wholesaler payment out of their bank account while waiting for payment from the PBM. Consequently, if you crystallize the role of pharmacies in this payment model, it would not be inaccurate to say that the pharmacies are in the business of loaning money to PBMs, at negative interest, for 45 days.

Quotable Thought

The current system forces pharmacies to accept lower reimbursements but has shown no impact on overall spending over the years.

The bigger challenge however, is that the interests of the patient become secondary to the interests of the payer or the PBM. The pharmacy benefit managers have discovered all sorts of ways to benefit from their middleman status, enhancing revenue for their company without necessarily adding a commensurate benefit to the patient. Their major claims of "cost savings" are a little disingenuous.

Pharmacy benefit managers claim to save the payers money by reducing the markup they allow each network pharmacy to charge. However, the payers have seen their costs rise virtually every year. And any cost savings that they may have incurred by squeezing the pharmacy payment is instantly offset when the manufacturer raises the wholesale price of the medication. Plus, the use of expensive brand-name drugs in mail-order PBM pharmacies often exceeds the amount used in community pharmacies because they have received incentives to feature a particular brand on their formulary. Clearly, the large benefit managers have become hugely profitable; it is not so clear that they have provided any benefit to the consumer.

And just think about this for a second. Since 1980 when the first third-party contracts were based on the average wholesale price of the drug, plus a dispensing fee of five dollars, the formulas have continually been lowered to the point where it is typically now average wholesale price (AWP)-15% plus a dollar. Pharmacies have been forced to accept lower and lower reimbursement per prescription every year, but it has had no impact on the rate of growth of expenditures on drugs by the consumers. While, paradoxically, drug price inflation for the past 30 years has run almost double the consumer price index.

Clearly, the 30-year history of third-party payments shows that attacking the reimbursement rates has not reduced the growth of spending. In fact, I could make the case that it has actually accelerated it. As a provider, if I am going to make less per transaction then the only way I can increase my sales is to do more transactions. This logic is irrefutable, and yet this silly notion that cutting reimbursements saves money continues to be debated.

What we do know is this: when real pharmacists help real people they save them real money. Hiding the true cost of a medication from the end-user behind a low co-payment and the relentless exposure to television and magazine advertising, has stimulated the overuse of expensive medications.

So why should you care about any of this if you don't own a pharmacy? Because the profitability of the profession is what funds job growth. No profits, no jobs, it is as simple as that. Less jobs available means lower wages for everybody over time. (At least in this segment of the market.) And it also means that store owners are looking for new ways to generate revenue which opens up an opportunity for you to fill that need.

The loss of profitability has made it very difficult for pharmacy owners to generate growth. They have tried to offer additional services, but it is challenging to have the clinical expertise in house to provide a full range of services expertly. If you provide mediocre services you actually end up hurting your customer engagement and customer loyalty. So again, I see this has a huge problem for store owners and a huge opportunity for pharmacists who want to develop specialized niche services.

The community pharmacist is a generalist. For the business to succeed she has to cultivate and develop relationships and build a strong perceived value for her business in the community. But to effectively monetize that customer base she has to be able to target groups of patients with appropriate services to solve their problems for them. It is just not possible to be an expert in multiple disease state services and aggressively manage a retail enterprise at the same time. The business of pharmacy has gotten too complex.

A few organizations have tried to offer services by partnering with independent pharmacies, but those organizations had questionable firewalls built to protect the owner from losing their customer base. No reasonable pharmacy owner trusts that allowing a PBM to deliver services to their patients will end well for their business. Since the FTC has allowed retail giants to own PBMs it is readily apparent that the firewalls between these PBMs and their retail stable mates are paper thin at best.

I see tremendous synergy for store owners to work with independent contractor pharmacists who are not affiliated with a competitive dispensing service. And I believe that sharing the revenue generated by any such activity is not only ethical but critical to the improvement of health care.

People will either find value in the service and pay for it or they won't. And that is how the market should work.

But once again, if you become a value trained pharmacist you will be able to develop a niche that creates value for your clients and income for you as well. The key issue for any health professional is that you must always act in the best interest of your patient. I believe that given our professional responsibility to act in the patient's best interest you should always make patients aware of a product or service that can help alleviate their pain and suffering. However, I also expect that you should never even think of selling products or services to patients that they don't need.

This is your challenge: 1)Stop complaining about the way things are and, 2) start creating a new patient care service you can co-market to pharmacy store owners. The single biggest untapped resource in our profession is the patient data housed in 20,000 independent drug store computer systems. Any store owner should be able to identify patients who need specialty treatments for asthma, diabetes, heart disease, anti-coagulation therapy or arthritis.

Wouldn't it be amazing if you could share the revenue you could create by serving these customers with a store owner? Most pharmacies still make most of their income on dispensing volume but need additional sources of income. And many clinically trained pharmacists don't want to be in the dispensing business but need access to patients if they hope to provide services. And don't forget that the key function of health care reform was to keep people out of the hospital. Doesn't it make sense that our residency trained clinical outpatient care specialists should relocate to a community setting?

This just makes too much sense to not get this done. So let me tell you about what is going on to address this challenge. There is an organization named The Community Pharmacy Enhanced Services Network: CPESN. They are building out a nationwide network of networks to leverage the power of pharmacists' patient care skills with a variety of payers. Once this network is built they are negotiating directly with payers to pay pharmacists to perform services in addition to dispensing medications.

I pulled the following quotes directly from their website so see if this value strategy sounds familiar. https://cpesn.com/what-is-cpesn

"Which pharmacies are ideal participants in CPESN? Pharmacies that focus on PATIENTS instead of PRESCRIPTIONS. Pharmacies that establish STRONG RELATIONSHIPS with their patients and members of the local health care community. Pharmacies that provide ENHANCED SERVICES. Services that transcend conventional requirements of an outpatient pharmacy program contract that are focused on improving clinical and global patient outcomes

Examples include: home delivery with patients status review, medication synchronization with clinical review, and adherence packaging with patient coaching. ENHANCED SERVICES address the unique medication use needs of complex patients, thereby helping them achieve the best possible results from medication use.

Through the provision of ENHANCED SERVICES, CPESN pharmacies are committed to improving HEALTH OUTCOMES and decreasing TOTAL HEALTHCARE COSTS for patients in their care."

This is exactly what I am talking about!

As you can see, the process of building professional networks is already underway. These networks need to be driven by patient care focused pharmacists and not bottom line driven business people who benefit from withholding care.

CPESN is building traction and I believe they now have chapters in at least 40 states. But again, I don't want to misstate what they are doing so I will quote directly from their website. They are a clinically integrated network.

"The term clinically integrated network is fairly new to the pharmacy industry, so there is a chance you might not have heard of it. A clinically integrated network is a collection of health care providers that demonstrates value to the market by working together to facilitate the coordination of patient care across conditions, providers, settings, and time to improve patient care and decrease overall healthcare costs.

It is meaningful because a clinically integrated network of pharmacists can engage with payers to receive a share of the dollars that payers save in patient care costs as a result of the services provided by the clinically integrated network."

To add additional weight and support to a network like CPESN, wouldn't it be awesome if we had a network of independent clinical contractors who could be hired to provide specialized care on demand for these pharmacy owners? Being able to provide value for others is the key to success. It always has been and always will be. The only time this fails to occur is when poorly designed public policy disturbs the normal working of a free market, value gets distorted and people get rewarded for behavior that produces waste or injury.

CHAPTER 5

Bad Economics

Non-value-trained pharmacists do not seem to understand practical economics. Let me give you an example of what I mean. Bad policy based on a misunderstanding of how economics works leads to bad results.

In 2002, our client base was virtually 80-85% senior citizens in Sun City, California. The local health maintenance organizations were able to offer a senior care HMO product that included a drug benefit. This drug benefit had a typical design with a five-dollar co-pay for generic drugs, and $20 co-pay for brand. However, due to Medicare funding rules, the HMOs in Riverside County were not going to receive the same level of funding as HMOs in other counties in 2003. This created an interesting laboratory to gauge the action of consumers in a real marketplace, rather than an artificially contrived one.

Prior to the new plan-year, the patient could get brand-name Drug A for $20 co-payment even though the real cost to the pharmacy was approximately $125 per month for 30 pills. Generic Drug B was available for a five dollar per month co-pay and a true plan cost of about $15. When we would talk to a senior and offer them a generic therapeutic alternative, they would say "No, I need my Brand Name Drug A."

After January 1 of that year, the HMOs dropped all brand-name drug coverage. What this meant for the consumer was that a drug that used to cost them $20 co-pay now converted to its real cost of $125 per month. Once the real costs were made apparent, the patients changed their tune. They preferred Drug A to Drug B when it was $20 versus five dollars, but not when it was $125 versus five dollars.

Economist eggheads can theorize and argue about this all they want, but the truth is, people will change their decision-making based on what it costs them to make a purchase. Making the cost artificially appear low to the consumer will artificially increase demand and drive incremental sales higher than they would be if the full price were charged to the consumer

Quotable Thought

Giving people the option of buying something for less than it's true price will stimulate them to buy more than they would if they had to pay the true price.

This also distorts the provider payment side as well. If providers get paid for withholding care and penalized for providing care eventually that is what they will do. If they get paid for providing service on billing code 12345 but not for billing code 6789 then eventually they will do a lot of the former and none of the later. There is a evidence that restrictive Medicare billing codes for ICD9 -10 primary care are a significant cause of the shortage of primary care physicians, because they simply can't get paid enough to cover the huge investment in their education. (See footnote at end of chapter)

Where does this leave the pharmacy industry? Interestingly enough the wholesalers and the retailers are seeing their margins squeezed relentlessly to the point that they continually have to find ways to operate more efficiently. At the same time, the middlemen have grown to bloated proportions.

Let me put it this way for you. Suppose there is a building in a distant town that houses 10,000 employees all making really good money. This big, shiny building and its business makes billions of dollars in profit each year in the healthcare business. And "*They*" work there.

Here is the gut wrenching truth. They treat no patients. They provide no care. They hold no hands. They wipe no tears. They pay no local taxes to your town. They provide no local jobs for your town. They create no local charities. And they have never comforted a grieving neighbor. Nor do they put up with invasive PBM audits that claw back dollars they have already spent.

What they do is take money from payers and trickle it down to providers. Somewhere between the payer and the provider a large percentage goes "missing." The pharmacy providers fund the drug purchase and loan this money to middlemen who used this money to build mail-order pharmacies and restrictive networks to take business away from the pharmacy providers and direct it to their mail order pharmacies.

The Federal Trade Commission has failed miserably to perform their mission which is stated on their website as: "Working to protect consumers by preventing anticompetitive, deceptive, and unfair business practices, enhancing informed consumer choice and public understanding of the competitive process, and accomplishing this without unduly burdening legitimate business activity."

But here is the real hot button. The payers for this activity pay them! They charge the providers to bill them, they get no-interest loans from the providers, they get huge rebates from the manufacturers, they overcharge the payers, and they make more money per transaction for funneling data than the providers do for doing all of the patient care work! And all of the real patient care service is provided by guess who--yes, the community pharmacy practitioner. Does that seem fair to you?

What if this same scenario played out in the inpatient arm of the profession as well? Oh, but is has. Driven by the Medicare payment systems, our hospitals have shifted from relying on pharmacy as a profit center to treating pharmacy as a cost center. Budgets are created and staffing levels are determined based on a formula predicting the patient census.

If the patient census exceeds the budget, it has become virtually impossible for the pharmacy director to get permission to hire more people because the pharmacy gets no internal credit for the extra services it is providing. Essentially, in most hospital systems, the pharmacy department generates no revenue line because they no longer bill for what they do, but simply perform to budget.

How Do You Communicate Your Value If You Can't Impact Revenue?

Many hospital pharmacists are attempting to demonstrate their value by computing dollars saved through drug stewardship or error prevention or re-admission prevention. But it is not clear how this is going to play out. All I can say for certain is, you need to be prepared to demonstrate your value if you expect to continue to get paid what you think you are worth.

The real problem is that because of the way many hospitals budget their revenue and expenses each year, demonstrating an internal cost savings or cost avoidance, does not necessarily transfer in to a real budget surplus. Those revenue dollars have likely already been allocated. And the other problem is that cost avoidance has a pattern of diminishing returns.

Cost avoidance will reap significant savings if hospital processes are inefficient or wasteful. However, once those processes are improved there will be less improvement or cost savings to be generated. If hospital pharmacies earn budget increases based on the amount of improvement achieved then how will they sustain this budget when there is no more improvement to make?

If you want to know why being recognized as official health care providers is such a big deal, it is precisely because a job that is solely a cost center has no ability to increase revenue. Therefore, it has no real power to control its own destiny. But remember what is doesn't have to always be. You can effect change if you understand value strategy. And you should fight tooth and nail to not allow people with little to no understanding of patient care to begin discounting your profession.

Quotable Thought

The single biggest failure of our profession over the last 40 years has been that we have allowed others to define our value in ways that have hurt our patients.

Pharmacy laws have not been able to keep up with the pace of change in the profession. Each state board of pharmacy regulates the pharmacies and pharmacists in their state. Many pharmacy laws were written during a time when pharmacists only worked in pharmacies. The Internet and websites were something boards were not ready to deal with. New laws had to be written.

Isn't it a bit absurd that a pharmacist in State A is legally prevented from counseling a patient in State B because they are not licensed in State B, when that very same patient can buy sketchy, unscientific and medically unsound advice from websites owned and operated by people with absolutely no professional medical training?

I get that no state board will give up the jurisdiction for the licensing and supervision of the pharmacists in their state. And I get that the role of the board of pharmacy is to more about protecting the public from malpractice than it is about promoting the value of the profession. But let's assume that the true goal of our profession is to improve the quality of our fellow citizens lives. How can you justify allowing health coaches, aromatherapists, holistic providers, and marketers to provide individualized health consultations to your citizens but you don't allow pharmacists who have passed a national licensing exam and completed a rigorous education to do so, just because they live in another state?

Is there not a way in which pharmacists could provide certain non-dispensing services to anyone in the country without having to maintain a license in each state? Pharmacies have to be licensed in each state to ship to residents in order to control the flow of dangerous drugs, but do we really need to regulate the flow of advice? Just think about this for a minute. Suppose you developed a great patient care service that you could offer using online consultation. Is it possible that the best way to avoid a conflict with the local state boards in each state would be to turn in your license in your home state so you could have the freedom to act as an unregulated health coach? Does that really make any sense for the profession or the health of this nation?

Having pharmacists practice pharmacy as independent contractors is something state boards need to prepare for. If we truly want to improve the health of this country, the boards of pharmacy need to help by modernizing regulations to allow pharmacist to practice their profession as healthcare consultants, health coaches and health care advocates without legal jeopardy of violating a practice act. Are the current regulations preventing or promoting the highest use of the talents within our profession to create maximum value for our health care stakeholders?

These are thought provoking questions with many possible answers. I challenge everyone in the profession to find the best answers for our stakeholders. There is work that needs to be done to make this succeed. Disengaged members of the profession will shy away from the work. Therefore, this problem is really an opportunity for you to become a pioneer in your field.

Footnote

Bodenheimer T, Berenson RA, Rudolf P. The Primary Care–Specialty Income Gap: Why It Matters. Ann Intern Med. ;146:301–306.

CHAPTER 6

Is there a Better Plan?

When providers get paid for doing stuff they will tend to do that stuff. If they got paid for preventing stuff they would tend to do that. Right now, providers mostly get paid for doing stuff. It is questionable whether all of that stuff is needed. Over 50% of the health care expenditures occur in the last six months of the person's life. Huge hospital expenses and expensive surgeries can dramatically raise the cost of the overall healthcare budget. Are all of these treatments truly necessary? Or is this an example of inefficient policy causing potentially "questionable" payments.

Senior Citizen Ping Pong

Let me give you a personal example of wasteful spending. When my father-in-law was nearing the end of his life, he was living in an Alzheimer's unit of an assisted living facility. Since assisted living facilities do not have licensed health care practitioners in California, such as nurses on staff, they are required by law to transport patients in distress to the hospital.

Despite having *Do Not Resuscitate Orders* on file the ambulance would pick him up and take him to the hospital. The hospital would then ignore the DNR order and bill $20,000 to $30,000 in services to Medicare to revive him, stabilize him and send him back to the assisted living a week later.

For two to three months this happened regularly until we finally had our local hospice group intervene in order to stop this madness.

With no quality of life for Grandpa and against the family's wishes, Medicare was billed for well over $100,000 that simply prolonged the inevitable by a few months. This bouncing of seniors from home-care to hospital occurs every day in America. Is this really the best use of public funds?

The Asheville Project in North Carolina and several other equivalent projects have demonstrated over and over again that pharmacist intervention in direct patient care saves the health-care system real dollars. A large chunk of these dollars come from eliminating expensive hospital visits and adverse drug events.

What Would True Health Insurance Look Like?

I believe it should look something like this. Health insurance would kick in when you needed a medical service that costs more than a figure such as $5000. What this means is that for routine checkups, routine prescriptions, first aid and urgent care type of treatments, insurance would not be involved. The responsibility for payment would fall back on the patient and the patient would be free to find the best available service for the best available price.

Employers could cost share this $5,000 with their employees by using health savings accounts. Employers could afford to do this because most employees would not need the whole $5,000 each year and the employer could buy stop loss insurance to cover anything that costs more than $5,000. This is the type of policy we used for the employees at our pharmacy and it dropped our benefit cost from $45,000 per year down to about $30,000 and we were able to cover every employee.

There will always be individuals that can not take care of themselves or have disabilities that prevent them from working. We need to provide that first $5000 through some specialized funding option such as a health savings account or direct cost share. However, the vast majority of people would have insurance to protect against a catastrophic event, but routine expenses would convert into cash purchases.

Overnight the cost of healthcare would decrease. Real competition would re-enter the market place. People would use the providers that gave them the best value. And people would only pay for what they needed or wanted.

Imagine the impact on prescription drug dispensing in this country if PBMs lost the ability to coercively direct patients in to mail order pharmacy! With over half of all dispensing occurring at mail order facilities, our most fragile population, senior citizens, are receiving the least direct contact with pharmacists in their community. Read this next paragraph very slowly and ask yourself, "Does this make sense?"

Quotable Thought

Our seniors, who have the most co-morbid conditions, and the least cognitive ability to deal with a complex drug regimen, are being mailed large bags of powerful drugs and being left on their own to figure out how to take it all correctly.

By the way, there is no control over whether those medications remained at safe temperatures throughout their journey to the patient's home. The temperature in a mailbox in the Southern California desert was easily over 160 degrees from May through October. Is this the best way to take care of our seniors?

I don't know if the politicians will ever have the stones to actually develop a truly market-based solution such as this but the inevitable side effect of high deductible policies would be to drive patients back to their local pharmacist.

This would engender an incredible opportunity for pharmacists to create valuable services for the patients they serve. And wouldn't it be amazing if all of those prescriptions currently being mailed were returned to our community run stores where the patient could actually obtain the benefit of a real relationship with a real pharmacist?

The High Cost of Bureaucracy

Let me share the story of the $1500 wheelchair. This is another example of how bureaucracy wastes valuable resources. My mother-in-law, Dotty, was in an assisted living home when she was 90 years old. She could no longer walk, so they called us and said they needed to get her a wheelchair. I said, "No problem, I know where I can buy a new wheelchair for about $100." They said "Don't worry, her Medicare will pay for it." So, they ordered her a wheelchair from a Medicare approved medical equipment supplier. She was not able to use her arms well so there was no need for a wheelchair she would have been fine with an even less expensive transfer chair. Nevertheless,they delivered a Medicare approved wheelchair to her. That was the last I heard of it until I was going through her papers over a year and a half later after she passed away.

Upon reviewing her Medicare benefit statements Medicare had paid to rent the wheelchair for 15 months at $85 dollars per month, for a total cost of $1275. Her 20% co-payment amount on the $1275 dollars came to $255.

Therefore, Dotty paid $255 in co-payments for a wheelchair when she could have bought for $99 in cash and the payer (you and I) paid $1020 for a $99 need.

If you are wondering why healthcare is so expensive Medicare is a large part of the reason. It turns $99 stuff into $1275 stuff. Without Medicare, the cost of this stuff would plummet. The way to get Medicare out of this debacle is to get them out of micromanaging healthcare. The reason the DME supplier had to rent the chair to Dotty instead of selling it to her was because Medicare rules mandate that procedure.

And this silliness plays out in every area of billing. Hospitals bill patients 10 to 15 times what stuff really costs because they only get paid for a small percentage of the service they actually provide.

A healthcare insurance plan that gives the consumer full responsibility for all routine purchases is the only health insurance payment model that will not bankrupt the nation. Therefore, I choose to believe that this model will eventually be adopted. Once it is adopted, then the pharmacy consumer will be back in play. No longer will the PBM and the insurance company be telling them where to go and who to talk to for routine services. Drugs and drug products would have to offer real dollar value for what they do.

Far too often new, expensive brand-name drugs are used for all the wrong reasons. If the patient is stable and controlled on a first-generation drug why do they need to be on the new generation drugs that cost 15 times as much? An insurance company who has a back-end deal to co-market a brand name drug has a different incentive than does a patient. The patient just wants to know how will it make them feel and how much it will cost? The PBM is trying to maximize their stock price and executive performance bonuses.

The moral of this story is that Congress as the stewards of the treasury need to show the people of this country that they are providing value to us. People get all worked up about politics. The D's don't like the R's and vice versa. But the reality is they have all done a poor job of spending our hard-earned money and we can not afford to borrow any more on foolish enterprises. This healthcare debacle can be fixed with a little common sense.

There are very interesting economically sound medical models popping up around the country that are challenging the traditional centralized, bureaucratic models prevalent since the advent of Medicare in 1964. Dr. Josh Umbehr of Wichita Kansas has pioneered a new patient-centered, fixed payment model for primary care that is beginning to catch on. His motto is insurance-free, hassle-free healthcare. His practice provides unlimited access to their physicians, extended time relaxed patient visits, same-day and next day scheduling services, house calls, a transparent full time access patient care electronic portal, diagnostic and procedures at no extra charge for a fixed fee between $50 and $100 per month depending upon a patient's age. You can check this out at: https://atlas.md/wichita.

The point I am trying to make is that we are not stuck with a stupid payment model unless we tolerate stupid payment models. Powerful moneyed interests spend lots of money in Washington, DC and the various state houses to perpetuate their own selfish interests. Regardless of your political ideology this has not worked out for the profession of pharmacy. The only true solution is to free up the intellectual capital to create innovative and effective patient care business models. Top down solutions are wasteful, inefficient, reduce the quality and availability of care, and have proven to be economically unsound everywhere they have been tried.

Pharmacists have let the system define their value and it has not worked out for us or our patients. Given the time and resources to do our jobs correctly overall costs would plummet. It is time that we put aside political ideology and adhere to the basic economic principals of supply, demand and opportunity cost. Designing a system with no cost to users and no penalty for bad choices is a recipe for financial disaster. The opportunity cost of misspending these resources will always lead to a unintended consequence.

There are many voices in this country seeking to divide us all in to warring camps. They do this to gain a political advantage for their party and gather power unto themselves. Rather than argue amongst ourselves about the issues on which we disagree, why don't we try rallying around the issues on which we all agree.

I think we can all agree that spending more than you bring in is a bad plan. I think we can all agree that our patients are not always getting the care that they need. I think that we can all agree that the local provider who best knows the patient is in the best position to create value and individualized patient care for that patient. And I think we can all agree that the providers who provide the care should be making more on the transaction than the paper pushers who have never met the patient.

I think the uniting force for our nation and for our profession is the concept of value. When politicians begin considering a policy change the current decision calculus appear to center around which big money donors are for it and which big money donors are against it. Policy seems to be driven by special interests that convince representatives to vote for or against a proposal based on how it will influence their party, their caucus, their career or their ability to get re-elected.

Why don't we try a novel approach that simply looks at the honest evidence of what the proposal is likely to do to create value for the people of this nation? Here y'all is the only strategy that really makes sense.

1. If the proposal creates value for the people of this country, then approve it.

2. If the proposal will undermine value for the people of this country don't approve it.

3. And if the proposal doesn't do either then table it.

I challenge my fellow pharmacists to demand that their representatives exercise the same logic when considering legislation that we do when making patient care decisions.

1. If what you are about to do will benefit the patient do it.

2. If what you are about to do will harm the patient don't do it.

3. And if it really doesn't matter then let the patient choose what to do.

Why should you care?

Regardless of your practice setting our profession is being strangled by a convoluted illogical health care system. Dietitians, nurses, chiropractors and others are health care providers, but pharmacists are not. The politicians threw the profession a bone by including medication therapy management in the Medicare legislation. However, they subsequently refused to pay for it or recognize pharmacists as health care providers. Go figure.

Department of Labor statistics show that 60+% of all pharmacists work in the community practice arm of the profession and less than 30% work in health systems. Undoubtedly then, the success of the community practice pharmacy businesses will have a huge impact on our profession overall.

With about 50% of all prescriptions being dispensed from mail-order facilities do you really believe that patients are receiving the level of care they deserve?

Adherence rates are horrible. Diabetes is skyrocketing. The population is obese. And there is a shortage of primary care providers because they can't get paid for providing primary care.

At the same time one of the leading causes of hospital admissions is medication misadventures. Pharmacists have the skills training, and ability to fix this problem for our nation. But we deserve to be paid for the value we create. Unfortunately that is a tough case to make when the data is against us.

Right now, community practice pharmacy is the most basic primary care provider in the nation. We see more people in any month than any other provider. Millions of people each day walk in to a pharmacy. In many cases, they are asking us to triage whether they can self-medicate or whether they require a doctor visit. If that isn't primary care I don't know what is.

Quotable Thought

While we profess to be an evidence-based profession why is it that we are so quick to cling to our biases rather than let the evidence guide our decisions?

We are in this together y'all. I realize that my hospital based clinical pharmacist friends are way better at what they do than I could ever hope to be. What I always tell them is that what they do is vital. But basically the patient is only in the hospital for a few days to a few weeks at most. They do a great job saving their life and getting them back home because they are experts at acute care. But the other 355 days a year they are in the community.

The good community pharmacist is an expert at community care. As a community based pharmacist I see my patients 4 times per month every month. I don't know how to do Vancomycin dosing and thankfully I don't have to. I am smart enough to send them to someone else when they need advanced care. But I do know my patients well enough to know when something is wrong with them.

I can tell when there has been a mood change or a change in gait. I can see mental confusion and dehydration. Through careful observation I can detect adverse drug reactions because I know my patients well enough to know that something is wrong. I help them manage their drug costs and make sure they are not victims of elder abuse.

A good community pharmacist has just as much or more impact on the patient's life as anyone else in the health care system. We just work on a different aspect of their lives than others do. Without us, all the good work my hospital-based colleagues do would go to waste. They would be right back in the hospital.

Quotable Thought

Based on the number of patient visits per month, community pharmacies are the largest providers of basic primary care in the country

Let's stand together and unite in the common interests of our patients. Our profession is poised to play a critical role in primary care and we won't get there by arguing who is more clinical than the other.

We won't get there on our clinical skills alone. We need to do a much better job of marketing our value to our stakeholders.

CHAPTER 7

The Final Act

Now, remember my progression for a good story, the set up, the problem and then the resolution? Here is where we come to the Third Act, the heroic solution. When this shift occurs, independent pharmacy will flourish in all its future forms.

A big reason people go where they go, and shop where they shop now, is because their insurance company tells them to. Once that is no longer the case, they will go where they get the best value.

Consider mail-order pharmacy. Mail order pharmacy exists today for one reason. It exists because the people who have control of prescription customer lives have provided financial incentives for patients to use mail order. The retail channel customer pays one co-payment per month; the mail-order channel customer pays two co-pays for three months. There is no way that mail order provides a better value for the patient without this financial incentive. They can get their prescriptions faster, for a lower incremental cost, and with better service at their local community pharmacy.

If patients truly want to avoid a trip to the pharmacy, there are plenty of pharmacies that will deliver to their home the same day they order without having to wait for an out-of-state mail-order delay of several days to a week.

Imagine a world where mail-order pharmacy loses this coercive financial incentive. Those prescriptions will flood back to the community. When they flood back to the community many patients will go where they get the best service. Where they will get the best service is most likely going to be the local community pharmacy. But in addition, well-positioned individual pharmacist VIPs will be able to provide direct patient care through a variety of unique new business models based in an on-demand community setting. Whether they work with other pharmacists to serve their patients or work with physicians offices and employers to provide medication management services they will be based outside of the hospital setting.

If we are going to actively compete and market directly to consumers then we have to understand how to compete. Unfortunately, one of the worst things the American educational system does is teach business skills. Teachers without any hands-on business experience struggle to explain the vital role that entrepreneurs play in society. They hope to inspire young people to create new products and services. But if they have never really done it, students never learn the skill.

That is why I have taken it as my personal mission to try to help fill this void in pharmacist training. I sold my pharmacy and ancillary businesses in 2007 to become a professor at a school of pharmacy. I did so in large measure because of my personal mission:

To instill the will to be great, the desire to excel, and the ability to create value, in the next generation of Pharmacists.

The secrets to successfully monetizing your professional skills are easy to explain when you have 40 years of experience actually doing just that. And that is what I propose to do in as many avenues as possible. I will include some key resources for you later in this book.

Ultimately, the answer to creating value for our patients is just not that difficult. I don't think the same way as a lot of pharmacists do and I concede that a lot of people in the industry may not agree with my point of view. But I think that the biggest thing holding back our profession is the lack of pharmacist training in the professional business skills they need to not just survive, but thrive.

And we don't have to come to general agreement or consensus to begin moving down a new path to success. The reality is that once the pioneers demonstrate the amazing power of building their own career value strategy, the rest of those interested will get on board. Being mired in a job where your company holds you in low esteem is a miserable place to be. Being successful and controlling your own destiny is a very energizing place to be.

Setting The Stage For Innovative Players

There was a time when all you had to do to open a successful pharmacy was find a good retail location and unlock the door. The population was growing fast enough that even if you didn't pick the best location in the world, enough people eventually came along and allowed the store to be successful.

Now we live in a time with restricted networks, universal Internet access, and global competition. And the practice of pharmacy has grown increasingly complex. In the traditional retail prescription dispensing model practice of pharmacy, an owner operator must now possess an elite set of skills if he or she hopes to be successful. These skills include strategic planning, business finance, accounting, human resources, strategic partnering, information technology management and legal compliance.

Unfortunately, management education is not as robust as clinical education in the schools of pharmacy. And corporate America has failed to fill the gap. Again, there was a time when it took pharmacists 5 to 7 years after starting work to earn a pharmacy manager slot. Now this just isn't true.

In the early 1980's, I was the training manager for Sav-on drug company and I developed and ran a three-day, 16-part course on pharmacy management that provided paid in-house education for our staff pharmacists who wanted to become managers. Today, these types of programs are few and far between.

In this new world in which we live, employers want dedicated employees with a managerial mindset but are not necessarily willing to pay for the formal training required to teach these skills. Thus, the default manner in which young pharmacists learn these skills is through trial and error.

If they are lucky enough to work with an excellent entrepreneurial pharmacist, they may learn to create valuable goods and services. However, it is difficult for a pharmacist who has only worked one or two places in their career to have the breadth of knowledge necessary to understand the wide range of skills required to perform at the peak levels of business efficiency.

The apprenticeship model simply does not work well for teaching management skills. I also believe that most non-fiction management books tend to be filled with puffery and self-congratulatory examples of all the great things the author did. And it is pretty difficult for the average reader to duplicate the author's success.

I believe in making the complex simple. I believe in learning the underlying principles that you can apply to make great real-time decisions. I believe that anyone who wants to succeed in their own business can be taught these principals in 6 weeks or so.

There is no excuse for failing to learn these important skills.

If you are lucky enough to work for an astute business person who understands all of this, then consider yourself fortunate and learn everything you can from him or her. But if you need a jump-start on your business training then consider some of the resources I will provide for you at the end of this book.

I am clearly not the only person who believes in the future of value-trained pharmacists. I have already told you about several awesome pharmacists who are actively engaged in helping pharmacists build their own business concepts. I am not saying I am the only or even the best choice for you to get connected to. But I am saying is that you need to find some guidance and start moving down the pathway to success. Staying where you are and doing nothing different, is not a great career strategy.

Quotable thought

Too many experts try to make life way too complicated. Albert Einstein said, "If you can't explain it simply you don't understand it well enough."

There are four areas in which you need to excel if you wish to own and/or operate a successful pharmacy related business or thrive as an employed pharmacist. If you understand the driving principles behind these processes you will always be able to fight through adversity and find a way to succeed.

These areas are:

1. Managing a value strategy, learning how to build a successful strategically sound business model;

2. Managing teams, learning how to build a high functioning team;

3. Managing the metrics, learning how to get the dollars to make sense; and

4. Managing Mindset, putting yourself in the right mindset to be successful.

These are the 4 core success skills. I believe it is the lack of these skills that causes 50% of all startup businesses to fail within five years. Once you understand these management skills you can easily learn to create your own thriving business niche that provides value to the customers you serve. Done correctly you will have more free time, more money and more freedom to practice the way you want to practice than you would working for someone else. One of the big challenges our profession must overcome is the ridiculous assertion that a pharmacist's value is tied to an hourly wage.

Your value in a transaction should be determined by the value you create for your customer. Your earnings should be a fair percentage of that value provided. Tying yourself to an hourly wage will never provide your family with the personal wealth you need to thrive in your retirement years.

CHAPTER 8
Lead Don't Follow

While most pharmacists possess the ability to master these skills, they lack the training in implementation, the hands on part of "getting it to work." This lack of training causes them to default to copying what someone else has done. Unfortunately, they are usually copying the wrong things from the wrong people and end up making the same faulty decisions that most people make.

In the 21st century, there is so much competition from so many global sources, that if you're not in the top 20% of thought leaders in your specialty it is highly likely that you will be invisible to the marketplace.

Think of the marketplace for VIP services as a Google search engine. A customer goes into this search engine and requests information about, "cures for fibromyalgia." If your cure doesn't show up on the first page of the search results, the chance of that person ever contacting you drops dramatically. Some people may scroll to page 2 but fewer people ever scroll to page 3 and hardly anybody goes any further. Therefore, in the real world marketplace, if you don't show up in the top of the search results for your chosen niche, it is going to be very difficult for you to attract any business.

A key element of positioning your business for success must be staking your claim to a large enough portion of the market to make a living, but not so large a market that you can't fight your way to the "top page" in the search.

Essentially, what this comes down to is that you must learn the following this:

1. How to decide what niche you want to own
2. How to compete successfully within that niche.
3. How to build a sustainable business model

But while strategic business planning to craft a business model that is likely to succeed is a huge ingredient in the recipe for success, it is just one part of that recipe. Ineffective management can still undo a fantastic business plan. Bad management is essentially the root cause of most business failures.

Customers, want to be treated well, with sincerity, and consideration. They want you to care more about them than anyone else. They want you to give them what they want, what they need and find a way to satisfy needs they didn't even know they had.

We Aren't The Only Profession In The Game

I will end this segment with a story to illustrate why this challenge is both important and time critical. In 2008 I traveled to Boston for my daughter's graduation from the Boston University School of Medicine's Masters in Behavioral Health program. As we were at the reception after the graduation ceremony I asked several of her classmates what they were planning to do with their new masters degree. The answers I heard were eye opening. They wanted to start weight management, diabetes management, healthy lifestyle management, smoking cessation, and stress reduction classes for patients.

What caught my attention was the fact that our school of

pharmacy was proposing our graduating pharmacists should undertake the same types of services. It occurred to me that historically, pharmacists have owned the field of dispensing and when a consumer thinks about drug dispensing they think pharmacy. But when you mention smoking cessation or weight control--who owns that market?

With so many players attempting to stake out niches in the healthcare marketplace, who is going to end up being a recognized provider of these services in the eyes of the public? The answer is up to you. If you don't claim the space someone else will.

I believe the advantage goes to the pharmacist who practices in a high-visibility, high traffic dispensing practice. By utilizing the demographic data provided by the prescription drug database, our new Third Act pharmacist hero, Gina, has two tremendous advantages in providing healthcare services over any other provider.

1. She has ready access to patient data -- she will know from their drug records what their health issues are.

2. These patients have a history of coming into her businesses and opening up their wallets.

A pharmacist, who would open up an office and call herself a service provider without being connected with the dispensing pharmacy, would have no stream of customers upon which to draw.

Having access to the customers, having an existing relationship with the customer, and having a customer predisposed to spending for what they want, is an incredible marketing advantage.

I realize that in many corners of the pharmacy industry, especially in academia, the drumbeat has been resonating for several years to get out of the dispensing business, but I believe that would be a tragic and fatal mistake for the profession.

Our current identity as a profession is rooted in the dispensing role. The public knows us and trusts us as dispensers of medications. This trust provides an incredible foundation upon which to grow additional services. The dispensing role creates points of contact with patients, access to their medication history and an opportunity to earn their confidence, and access to patient care.

Quotable Thought

Access to patient data and the encounter history with that customer is a key advantage to leverage toward development of new services

Trying to make the public recalibrate their image of the pharmacist as a quality option to become their primary caregiver without leveraging the role of the dispensing pharmacist as a base, would be folly and economic suicide. Attempting to dramatically change a strong brand identity is very risky.

The critical skill you're going to need for success in the next phase of the pharmacy business cycle is the ability to create value for your client.

What is exciting is that there are broad ranges of clients that can be served! Traditional pharmacy education focuses on patient care, but that is just the tip of the iceberg. Individual VIP Pharmacists are already exploring and testing new and exciting opportunities. In addition to providing creative patient care services, pharmacists have developed disease management services, consulting practices, software, creative compounding practices, wound care companies, bio-identical hormone replacement management practices, nutritional practices and many other niche services.

One Big Idea That Needs To Be Dealt With

Collecting, analyzing, interpreting and reporting data is going to be a critical battleground in the next twenty years. There is much current talk about Star ratings and networks of pharmacies being based on performance in achieving health outcomes. But here is the critical piece of all this you must understand. Whoever controls the data will control how it gets reported. Therefore, "He who controls the data will control the doling out of the rewards."

Those of us who practiced before computers were prevalent (think before 1985) can reflect on the loss of control that happened when PBMs began to control the data. If you have a skill for data management now is the time to begin developing systems for using data that will enable pharmacists to prove their value. If other entities such as PBMs control that data, there is no telling what the data will say. History has proven that non-pharmacists don't value what we do as much as our patients do. No one can predict how all the political battles will eventually manifest into a new payment model for pharmacy services. But if you believe that someone else is going to do the hard work to make sure your interests are protected, then you have not been paying attention to reality.

Quotable Thought

The only way you can insure that you will have gainful employment in the future is to make sure that you can do something that someone is willing to pay for.

Right now, there are lots of good jobs in dispensing, clinical practice, industry and academia. But the jobs of the future are going to be different. And the only way you are going to be able to compete for those jobs is if you stay alert for opportunities, keep honing your skills and learn how to create value for the stakeholders you want to serve. In short, you must become a VIP.

Becoming a Valuable Innovative Pharmacist will be the key to long-term career success in your chosen niche. Once pharmacists are unshackled from traditional business models, pharmacists can begin to work in entirely different ways. They will work as free agents not attached to a single employer. They will not be automatically tied to pharmacies or the restrictive corporate policies of their employers.

Driven by the prominence of the Internet over the past 30 years, unique practice models have developed where pharmacists set their own hours, work from home, and serve clients from remote locations. And this trend will continue to grow.

I believe that a free-agent nation of valuable innovative pharmacists, with well-developed specialty business models, will partner with dispensing pharmacies and community based medical practices to provide an expanding array of unique services to healthcare consumers.

The sky is the limit and the opportunity is now. If you don't like the way you are practicing now, then stop fretting, and start your own independent practice. Find a problem, develop a solution, deliver on your promise and control your own destiny.

CHAPTER 9

How to Create a Value Strategy

"The man who will use his skill and constructive imagination to see how much he can give for a dollar, instead of how little he can give for a dollar, is bound to succeed." Henry Ford

A critical step in developing a good business model is creating a sound value strategy. You can be the smartest person in the world but if your business strategy doesn't resonate with the market you will not succeed. Regardless of the strategy, successful businesses need to be able to do three things well to consistently develop and compete in the marketplace.

1. Identify a pain in the marketplace. What do customers say is missing? What do they want and would gladly pay for if somebody would just give it to them? Identifying this pain in the marketplace allows you to craft a strategy to fulfill that need, which will energize your growth and catapult you into a market share position.
2. Develop a solution to remedy that pain, to ease that pain, or to fill that market void. There are lots of ways you can craft a solution for the marketplace. However, if you don't understand what the true drivers of purchase behavior are, no strategy is likely to succeed. Thus, understanding what really drives purchase behavior or the decision to buy is also critical.
3. Make an offer to your target market. The one piece of the puzzle that many people forget is that you have to put your offer in front of the customer.

You have to offer the solution that people want to have. If you never make an offer you will rarely get paid.

Those three challenges - identifying a market, developing a solution and offering to perform - require a business plan that will adhere to these three standards. Businesses that resonate with the marketplace and grow quickly follow this simple process. Of course, there are numerous other challenges along the way. You need to be able to scale and grow the business. You want to protect your idea from theft, and your business model has to earn a profit.

However, the essential driver of a successful strategy is understanding, why people buy what they buy and conversely, why people don't buy what they don't buy. In addition, what would make them buy what you offer instead of what somebody else is offering? Fail to understand this and success is unlikely.

I believe there are really only three things you need to know about what drives people to make a purchase, use your service, or select what you have to offer instead of what your competition offers. I published an article in the journal, *Research in Social and Administrative Pharmacy* titled, "The Value Prescription: Relative Value Theorem as a Call to Action," in the summer of 2011, describing this process as the Relative Value Theorem. These three elements are depicted graphically in the figure on page 106. It shows how Price and Service interact through the prism of Perceived Value to help a buyer make a purchase decision.

The first and most recognizable element, of course, is the price. What does it cost? But be careful not to equate this strictly with the dollars and cents. Let me explain what I mean. If two items are identical and they're both offered at the same price – let's say that price is $29.95 - that does not mean that those two items cost the same. Because included in the price/cost calculation for this service is not just the dollars and cents I have to part with, but the energy I have to expend, the time I have to put into it, the emotional drain it costs me to buy from you. All of the costs in time, energy, enthusiasm, money and effort go into the component that I'm describing as price.

In other words, what it costs me to buy your product is not only the dollars that come out of my bank account. It is also the time it takes me to go to your store to pick it up, the gasoline it costs me to drive over there, the aggravation I have to experience waiting in line at your business, and the annoyance I get when it's not ready yet and I have to come back multiple times. The opportunity cost of what I could've been doing with that time rather than sitting around waiting in your stores is also part of the price.

Multiple factors go into the price of your service. Understanding that price is one element critical to your development of a solution to ease a pain in the marketplace. How can you craft an offering that your targeted customer will calculate as being lower-cost?

There are different ways to accomplish this task. The most obvious is the Walmart Strategy, where it costs them less dollars out of their bank account. That's the traditional discounting approach. Essentially, Walmart says to their targeted consumer, "We're going to offer everything at the lowest out of pocket cost, and therefore, you know when you go to Walmart that you're going to get a lower price." That's their marketing strategy. It's been very effective for them.

But I would argue that this is probably not the right strategy for a locally owned independent business, primarily because it's very difficult to pull off. There's only one way you can be the low-cost leader, and that's to sell everything at the lowest price. In order to be able to sell everything at the lowest possible price, you would need to wring all non-essential costs out of your business model.

To buy everything at a better cost, to be able to sell it at a lower price, requires leverage with suppliers. To operate at the lowest operating costs requires high sales volume and inexpensive labor and rent. Those are not things that the typical small business can pull off. Pursuing a low price strategy may actually be counter-productive. If you call yourself the low price leader and a customer checks only to find out that you are more expensive, you will have driven a wedge of mistrust into your relationship. Customers will begin to doubt you. They won't trust you. They won't come back.

Consider this: if every competitor had this same strategy in a competitive marketplace, only one company could possibly be telling the truth. The rest would essentially be lying to their customers. The Walmart strategy is available, it is just very difficult to execute. Fortunately, there are other strategies available to small businesses.

A small local business can make the argument that it costs the consumer less time and energy, gasoline or effort to shop at the local option rather than drive the extra ten miles to go to the big-box store. That is another way to influence the price element of the Relative Value Theorem. If you apply your knowledge of all the elements that factor in to the cost, other than just the dollars spent, several other options become clear. Other questions a business can pose to identify the true cost drivers for their product or service are:

1. How many times do you have to go back to the store to get your order completed?
2. How long do you have to wait in my store versus their store?
3. How easy is it for you to get in and out of the store? (This is hugely important for people with limited mobility).
4. Do you feel welcomed and appreciated?
5. Is the business process user friendly and stress free?

If the small local operator saves the customer effort or money in another area by offering extra services that save money, they can promote this price advantage. Eventually the customer evaluates your price offering as the sum of dollars that comes out of her bank account and the combined other costs to her in time, energy, aggravation and effort. Deciding how to position your product or solution in the marketplace clearly requires a sound pricing strategy using this complete definition of price.

Now, what happens if the only marketing strategy you do have is price? Well, the easiest thing for a lousy competitor to do to attract new business is to lower their price. That competitor may be able to lower that price to a level that is unprofitable for you. Bad companies mistakenly believe that they can lower prices below profitability to attract customers, and then eventually raise the price up to where they'll be profitable.

In any marketplace, there's always a competitor that tries a lower price as their strategy to increase sales. However, it's a very difficult strategy to pull off and stay profitable over the long haul unless you continually improve efficiency. To say you are, in fact, going to be the low price leader all the time on all items is risky. As soon as you're not, you will lose the customer's trust.

Apparently, Walmart can't even make the Walmart Strategy work on all product categories. There is too much competition from too many different distribution channels. It is significant that Walmart changed their slogan from "Always the Low Price Leader" to "Always Low Prices" in 1988, and then in 2007 changed their slogan again to "Save Money, Live Better."

Once an item sells strictly based on its price, whoever has the lowest price gets the sale and whoever doesn't have the lowest price doesn't get the sale. That item then becomes a commodity. When you look at a business strategy for an individual business owner or an individual professional, becoming a commodity is not going to be a long-term successful strategy. Someone else will always offer it cheaper.

So while price is important, it's clearly not the only thing that drives business. If it were, then only the business with the absolute lowest price would stay in business. Everybody else would do zero sales. I've never found any market where that's true. There's clearly something else at work here. The exception proves the rule. A simple example of the price rule not being perfect is that one company sells a set of four tires for $300 and another sells that identical set for $350, the company charging the higher price is still doing some business. So what is that other element that is important?

The second element is service. What else do I get with the product in addition to the product itself? What side benefits do I get with a purchase from you in addition to just purchasing the product? Well, what exactly does this term "service" mean? The service component of an offering is everything that comes with the product over and above the product itself. In other words, if I'm offering to fill your prescription for a $10 co-pay, the $10 co-pay is the price, and you're getting a filled prescription for that. The other things that you might get from me, such as personalized service, free home delivery, expert consultation, a friendly face, a neighborly atmosphere in the store, those are things that are not exactly part of the product. They're additional add-on features, benefits, or services provided by my system of selling you this product.

The component of service adds a new layer of complexity to the purchase decision. What we'll see is people might say, "Well it's cheaper to go over there. That guy sells it for $2.00 cheaper, but when I come in here, they know my name, it's always ready, they give me great advice and they help me pick out my over-the-counter medications that go along with the prescription. These extra services are worth something to me. Therefore, even though the price is a little bit cheaper somewhere else, I'm going to patronize this particular pharmacy because I like what else they have to offer."

That is the essence of a service offering that you have to design as a business owner and as a marketer. You have to observe the marketplace and be aware of current trends. You have to know what's going on. You have to know what people are charging for things. You have to know how your competition conducts their business and how they present their offering to the public.

1. Are they a high-service, high-touch business?
2. Are they a low-cost leader, low-service business?
3. What do your competitors do that irritates customers?
4. What do they do that customers rave about?
5. What can you offer that they can't or won't?

These are all things that you have to understand about your competition to know where to position your business to attract the level of market and level of customers that you want. To understand how to create value for a customer, you clearly have to comprehend the pricing component and understand the competitive service offerings.

Are price and service all that goes through people's heads when they decide to buy something? If it was strictly price and service, then the person with the lowest price and the best service, theoretically, should have all the sales. What we see in the real marketplace is different. There is not one business that just dominates every single sale within a marketplace. So what is this other element that goes into deciding why we buy something? I will use an example of a car purchase here to make my point.

When I was a starving student, didn't have any money, living on student loans trying to get my degree, I bought a 1963 Chevy Impala for $150. It was the lowest priced thing I could get. It ran and that was about all that I was concerned with. I needed something to get from point A to point B. As I progressed in my career, got a job and started making a decent living, that car was no longer acceptable as a vehicle for my needs.

It still drove. It could still get from point A to point B, but it was no longer something that I wanted to have. I wanted something a little sportier, a little fancier. When I went back to my reunion with all my high school buddies, I didn't want to be driving a '63 Impala. I wanted to be driving a new car. Why? Because I wanted to show some outward sign that I was doing okay, and rolling up in a '63 Impala with a dented fender wouldn't have projected the image that I was looking to project - that I was now fairly successful.

Obviously, the price was cheaper for a '63 Impala than for a 1980 BMW 320I. The Impala required no down payment and no monthly payments. It didn't have high insurance. It didn't have high repair bills or a lot of the baggage that came with the new vehicle. It was certainly more expensive to drive a brand new 1980 BMW than a paid for '63 Impala. The other element that makes the difference for buyers is something called perceived value.

1. How does the purchase made me feel?
2. Does it allow me to project the image that I want to project?
3. Does this purchase satisfy a need that has nothing to do with the transaction, but everything to do with how I perceive myself as a consumer, businessman, family person and leader?

As I progressed through my career, having a nice car was more important than having a cheap car. Not everybody would make that same decision, but the reality is that the third element, perceived value, does factor in to the purchase equation. In addition to the price and service, people do indeed consider the perceived value of the purchase. Thus, the third element that helps people decide what to buy is perceived value.

1. How does it make me feel?
2. How badly do I want it?
3. How much do I wish to own that vehicle?
4. How much does it project the image I want to project?

A buyer may wish to buy a nice dress. She may be able to find a nice dress at either Nordstrom's or Target, but she might not shop for that dress at Target because she wants to be able to tell her friends she bought the dress at Nordstrom's. One element of the purchase decision will always be the perceived value of the purchase.

The perceived value is going to vary by individual. If she can't afford to buy it anywhere else, and even though she would really like to buy it from Nordstrom's, she still may not do it. She might love to be dressed in all Nordstrom's clothes, but if she doesn't have enough money in her budget, she has to seek less expensive options. Those are not good/bad or a right/wrong decisions. What they are is the real world intervening with your perceptions and desires.

So when you're crafting and developing a solution to the marketplace, the first thing you have to understand is that no single offer is going to appeal to everybody. Secondly, you need to understand that even though buyers may want what you have to offer, they may not be able to afford it right now. One of the biggest mistakes novice business owners make is to overestimate the market response to their offer. They become disappointed when they don't get rich overnight. They build their fixed expenses faster than the potential revenue that can support these expenses, but please, don't get your spending ahead of your sales.

There's only one way that you know how the market is going to respond to your offer and whether or not that offer is going to be successful: by putting the offer out there. You may think you've come up with the best price, and you may think you've crafted the best service and benefits around your product. But the marketplace may react entirely different, because you misread the perceived value of this.

Let me give you an example: our drugstore in Sun City, California serviced a town of about 15,000 people, mostly senior citizens, many of whom required incontinence supplies to be an aide to their daily living. At the time, a pack of 18 adult diapers cost $12.99 and somebody who needed them might go through 2-3 diapers a day. For people living on a fixed income, this was a significant expense. I looked out to the marketplace and saw a large block of people that needed the product. I saw some of the embarrassment they felt when they had to go into the store and buy these products. I saw that diapers were fairly expensive at $13 for 18 for a 5-6 day supply; so $13 for 5 days means every month they're spending $78 to buy diapers.

My rational brain said that if I could figure out a way to lower the cost and to make it easier to purchase those diapers that would be a wonderful addition to the marketplace and would be successful. I spent quite a bit of time finding a resource that could maximize efficiencies in the purchase. Instead of having one bag of 18, I could get a box of 72 diapers for a substantially lower cost per diaper. I negotiated a low enough cost from the distributor to allow me not just to buy the product cheaper, but to actually ship and deliver the product directly to someone's home.

My guess was that if they didn't have to go out and make that embarrassing purchase, and if I could ship the product at a lower price than they could buy off the shelf, that I would corner the market on adult diapers.

I reviewed competitive prices and my product was cheaper. I looked at the quality of the product, and my product was just as good. I looked at the extra benefits of home delivery. Some of these folks weren't driving any longer so they had to walk over to the store. I thought it would be an advantage not having to carry these big bags of diapers all the way home.

So what happened? Well, I put this offering out to the marketplace, I promoted it for several months, and basically had

3-4 people that signed up and took advantage of it. After investing $4,000-5,000 in advertising and getting only several hundred dollars in sales as a return, I started thinking, "What's gone wrong?"

I started talking to customers and saying, "How come you don't think this is a good deal?" And the response surprised me. They said, "I can't afford to spend $70 for a box of diapers. I can spend $13 every five days, but I don't have enough to spend $70 once per month to get the same amount of diapers."

So it was a cash flow problem. If I had asked my customers before launching, I would've known about this hurdle before I wasted all the time and energy building the product and devoting time and energy to the concept.

In reality, my pricing was better, the service offering of home delivery was better. But the perceived value of saving $8 every month to get home delivery was not. The customer's thinking was, "I can't afford to give up the extra cash out of my bank account. It's not worth the risk to me, because I might have something that comes up that I need to spend that money on."

It was really a cash flow issue. I learned very clearly that it's not just price, service and benefits; it also includes the filter of the individual consumer's perceived value. And that perceived value is not limited to merely whether or not I want it. It's going to be whether I can afford to do it. The individual perceived value calculation analyzes how this offer compares to all the other potential uses of my money.

One of the biggest mistakes a lot of entrepreneurs make, is looking at your product or service offering only in the realm of competing with other similar product offerings. I was looking at adult diapers and comparing it to all other sources of adult diapers. The customers were comparing it to other uses of their money.

When we think we are selling over-the-counter vitamins, the consumer is actually saying, "I've got $30 to spend. I can spend it on vitamins, I can spend it on a movie, I can spend it on going out to dinner, I can spend it on a book, I can spend it on a doctor's visit or I can spend it on ice cream." For them, the value equation is determined by comparing what you're selling to all alternate uses of their time, energy and money. This one single understanding changed my life as a marketer, because I began to understand the real motivations that cause people to buy or not buy.

At this point, what you need to internalize is that there are three things that people use to decide whether or not they're going to buy your product or service.

1. What is the price/cost in time, money, and energy for me to buy the product?
2. What are the services and extra benefits I get from buying the product from choice A versus choice B versus choice C?
3. How badly do I want or need this product, and can I afford to use my limited amount of money to buy this product versus all other options I have for spending that money?

The essence of creating value for your customers is learning how to modify your price and service offering to compete in the marketplace of competitive offerings within your target market. You must also enhance the perceived value of your product compared to all other uses of their money.

As a business person, the only thing under your direct control is the price and service offering. The perceived value component is internal to the person or organization making the decision to buy. If you want to be effective as a business person, I suggest that you spend a lot more time up front understanding the purchase motivation for your potential customer before you waste time on the price and service. Successful entrepreneurs understand how these three elements interact, unsuccessful people always seem to leave one out of the discussion and pay for it.

The lucrative opportunities in the marketplace come when you find a pain in the marketplace. This pain represents a demand or unmet need in the marketplace which potential purchasers are begging you to fill. Once you develop a solution to ease that pain, the customers will be primed to buy. Your marketing is much easier and much more successful when customers are standing in line to buy your product before you even open for business. Pre-selling the market builds demand. The last remaining hurdle to success is to simply make the offer to sell.

The novice business person thinks along a linear pathway: develop a product, market the product, and sell the product. The experienced marketer thinks in reverse order. They figure out what people are aching to buy, and then find a way to sell it to them. If you train yourself to think backwards and find out what consumers want to buy first, you can develop a solution to the pain in the market that will appeal to that market segment's internal motivation to buy. Developing a product that meets the needs of a hungry market will greatly improve your chance of success.

A hungry market waiting to pounce on a viable solution will speed the rate at which your offering will be purchased. Marketing that offers a solution to a pre-sold market is virtually guaranteed to succeed. If you have crafted the offer correctly and you've developed a solution that meets the internal motivational needs of the purchaser rather than the procedural needs of your business, you are much more likely to make the sale.

Because most marketers and most business people fail to perform their research correctly at the beginning, there are always opportunities to develop products and services that appeal specifically to people ready to buy the solution. These can be sold without expensive marketing efforts, because the market is already searching for your solution. Your competition will wonder why and how you got the order when they've been trying to sell their solution for years. Answer the internal motivation question first, and then design the solution is the pathway to financial freedom.

Allow me circle back to the issue of how people decide what to buy. The unimaginative business discounts their price as their marketing strategy. A smarter business thinks backwards to identify a hungry market. A key advantage of the backwards development of a product is the market is focused on the solution, not the price. A hungry market understands what the lack of a solution is costing them.

If a customer is spending $1 million a year because they can't resolve a shipping problem, and you can resolve that shipping problem for them by offering a service that removes their main roadblock, what is that service worth to the potential purchaser? It's worth at least $1 million per year! And you may be able to provide that service for something substantially less than that.

Pharmacists need to stop thinking in the dollars per hour mindset.

To build a successful value strategy for your business you must understand,

1. What the real motivation for your buyer is,
2. What the real costs to that business are,
3. How much money your solution will save your client, and
4. How much more money your client will earn with your solution.

Then, and only then, can you offer a solution that either saves them money, earns them more money, or eliminates a big opportunity cost for them. And you can do that in a way where you've now shifted the buyer-seller discussion from, "how does your offer compare to your top three competitors" to "based on what your business does, I would be crazy not to use your service" The net result of the purchase of your product or service must be a high perceived value to the customer.

Let me be clear on that. Suppose, in trying to sell your service, you say, "My service costs $500 a month, and I will do XYZ, and from XYZ you're going to get the following benefits." What you're asking the purchaser to do is think about that. Then calculate where he is going to get the $500 a month. Then decide whether or not that $500 a month is going to give him anything in return. Clearly it's good for you, since you get $500, but he may not understand or see what that $500 a month is going to get for him.

So flip that discussion on its ear. Your purchaser is spending $5,000 a month to do a particular thing. You come in and say, "I know that you're spending $5,000 per month on this. We're going to take all of this headache away from you and we're going to do it for $2,500 a month." What does that purchase cost your purchaser?

It costs him an improvement of $2,500 a month, which means he'd be crazy not to buy your solution if it works.

Which of those offers do you think is more likely to be successful?

1. Pay me $500 a month and try to figure out what it's worth for you to work with me, or
2. I will save you $2,500 a month if you use my service.

The secret to small business success is that you need to be responsive to the needs of your client at a level the big businesses just can't, because nobody's paying attention to it at this granular level. Where you can succeed and where you're going to thrive as a small business person is by:

1. Identifying a pain in the marketplace,
2. Crafting a solution to ease that pain and then,
3. Crafting an offer to be put in front of people that is a clear win for them.

When you do that, you can be on your way to having a successful business model. Once you understand how value is created, you need to begin crafting a strategy that has a good likelihood of succeeding in creating value in the mind of your targeted consumer. There are a few things that I need to explain further. When you are a business owner, you set the tone for that team. You must decide what you want your team to be known for. A good value strategy involves aligning your business principles and your core set of beliefs with your business model, so that everything that you do resonates with your core values. If my business is a high-touch, high-service, take care of the customer kind of business, then I have to design business systems that make sure that I execute on that promise.

You cannot be the low price leader, eliminate all the extra payroll from your workflow, have just-in-time delivery of your product and also say you're going to give the highest level of personalized service. The two concepts do not match; they can't match, because you have to build the team differently. You have to build your workflow differently. You have to build your customer service strategy differently based on your core values. Defining yourself as the low price leader comes with a whole set of continual activities to maintain that value.

Considering yourself a high service, hands-on, meet-every-need-that-you-have kind of service provider means that your system must support that mission. Your people have to be trained to do that. Your policies and your staffing levels have to be higher. You might have to pay people a little more because you want people that can execute your vision every single time, not just when they feel like it. So there's an entire value strategy that you have to align with. Regardless of which strategy you choose as a business, there are three things that you have to do in order to make sure that you have the internal resources and competencies to pull off your strategy.

First, you must examine the core values that you believe in and build a strategy that resonates with your core values. The reason this is so critical is that, over time, based on the daily activities, based on the practice, based on your management style, a team always assumes the personality and demeanor of its leader. If you are a fun-loving, outgoing, casual, personal, very hands on coach, the team's going to act differently than if you're a restrictive, autocratic, follow the rules, scream and yell kind of leader. If you try to be someone you are not, it never seems to work out well in the long run.

To build a value strategy plan that works you must match the business model with your natural style. You may think that you can change your natural style, but I have never seen it happen. If strategically you want to develop a high touch, high service business, but your basic core values are always to find the lowest cost, cheapest deal available, you will have a problem staying with the high touch strategy over the long haul. If you are someone that believes in cheap, cheap, cheap, it's really hard for you to turn your head around and say, "I have to hire better people. I have to give more hours. I have to put an extra person here, because our lines are getting too long at a certain time of the day."

On the other hand, some leaders say, "Regardless of cost, I think we get a payoff by having an excellent customer interface and a real strong customer experience. It may not make dollars and cents today, but it's going to expand my business and increase my referral capacity. I'm going to get more customers over the long haul because they're going to tell their friends how great we do in customer service." You must align your inner beliefs with your business strategy. You can't mix and match styles without causing a problem.

If you honestly believe that one strategy is better than the other, and you don't have the core values it takes to pull it off, it doesn't mean you can't build a value strategy around it. However, it does mean you need to put someone on the operations management team who has those skills and mindset and will execute this vision and keep it on track.

The second thing that you absolutely have to do is align the style with your strengths. Once you've decided on a strategy, then all your business practices, all your hiring practices, all your training practices, all the discipline of your employees must align with that style, must encourage that style, must reward people that do it well and correct people that do it wrong.

If you allow people within your workflow not to do what you want them to do, then by default, you're not going to execute on that promise. You're not going to go out to the marketplace and say "here's what we do" and have customers come in and actually get that experience. If you advertise that you are a high service business, and then customers come in and wait in long lines and get bad service, the customers will be disappointed. They won't trust you. They will leave and find someplace else to spend their money.

If you market high service, and they receive great service, they will instantly recognize the difference between you and your low service competition. They will be much more likely to say, "Wow, this is cool" and tell their friends. The challenge is to constantly review your hiring practices, your workflow, your scheduling and your layout to make sure that you're executing on your promise. You need to religiously do everything you can to align your daily actions with your strategy.

And third, you have to select the right people to be on your team. Basically you have to cast your play to include the right actors. You must find people who believe that your strategy is the right way of doing it. You must be able to trust that their core values are aligned with the values and core beliefs of your business. If they are not, you need to determine quickly if they never will be or if they will respond favorably to additional training.

This is a tough call sometimes, but in my opinion, if after two weeks a new employee cannot get aligned with your style of business, they're never going to get aligned. That's when you need to decide who wins the part in your play. If two weeks into rehearsals, the bad actor wants to play Shakespeare with a German accent when you require an English accent, then you've got to find a different actor. That's just the way it goes. Savvy business owners ruthlessly protect their core values by quickly getting rid of outliers and by educating those that can improve. Knuckleheads bring in the wrong people, put them in the wrong jobs, and then blame it on the employee when it doesn't work out.

Interestingly enough, when you allow somebody to stay in your system who doesn't follow the rules you have set, you create a mismatch between what you say you want and what you demonstrate that you allow. When that happens, you have defeated the entire strategy. The people who believed you and bought in say, "Well, he doesn't really mean it." The people that never bought in and don't want to do it say, "So I can get away with whatever I want," and you've just destroyed the capability of your team to deliver on their promise.

Contrast that with "We've hired a new person. We've told them how we want it. We've modeled how we want it. They refused to do it so we removed them." That's one more reminder for everybody on your team that "You see? She believes it, she means it." If you don't do it the way we do it here, then you're free to go do it somewhere else.

An essential element of success for your value strategy is aligning your goals, core values, strategy and work habits to excel at the way you want to operate. Once you've decided on your strategy, and which stakeholders you're going to serve, the next step is building a team that has the skills you are likely to need in the full range of situations your team might face.

An example of where pharmacists must demonstrate their value is the issue of medication adherence.

Adherence is defined as "the extent to which patients take medications as prescribed by their health care providers" With the heavy emphasis the profession has focused on medication therapy management and patient counseling over the last decade, one might assume that a majority of patients would be adherent with their medications. Unfortunately, that is not the case.

Poor medication adherence in the treatment of chronic diseases is a serious problem. The total cost of suboptimal medication adherence has been estimated at $177 billion annually in total direct and indirect health care costs (NCPIE, 2007). This is a huge target of opportunity for the profession to advance the narrative of pharmacist value.

Pharmacists must learn to create value by engaging with patients to such a degree and in such ways that patients embrace medication adherence as something truly 'valuable' (High Perceived Value). It is not enough for a us to know clinical therapeutics and applied pharmacology. Pharmacists must be able to motivate patients to achieve desired outcomes. Clinical knowledge is critical but understanding how to create value for our stakeholders is equally important. By utilizing the RVT, pharmacists can understand how to better motivate stakeholders to become healthier.

Consumer purchase decisions are driven by perceptions of the value of what they are offered. When thinking about patient decisions to "purchase" medication adherence services, pharmacists must learn to ask the right questions and listen to patients to the answers to understand their reluctance to take their medication correctly. To those of you who are familiar with Dr. Bruce Berger training on Motivational Interviewing (www.mihcp.com) I suggest that in your attempt to build rapport with the patient and then address their real issues, you might find that value theory can help guide this discussion to identify some of the true barriers to effective utilization of drug therapy.

1. Are they able or willing to spend the money, time or effort on their medications or adherence (P)?
2. Do they understand what they are getting for their time, money or effort (S)?
3. Do they even value their medication therapy (PV)?

While the logical side of the mind computes the price and service components, perceived value is controlled by the emotional areas of the brain. An adult male patient may to refuse to take blood pressure medications because he believes the side effects can negatively impact sexual performance. For some people, the perceived value (PV) of male pride can be much more of a motivator than the risk of a heart attack (S).

Who can be served?

The process of developing patient care services that will succeed in a competitive marketplace requires pharmacists to apply the concepts inherent in the relative value theorem. Given the realities of a market-based economy, the transition from fee for service dispensing to value based patient care services, a tight job market and healthcare reform, all pharmacists will need to sharpen these skills to remain competitive. To continue to get paid a competitive salary, pharmacists will need to demonstrate that they can create value for at least one of the stakeholders in the healthcare market place.

Health Care Industry Stakeholders

There are five types of potential clients with an economic, clinical or humanistic stake in the healthcare marketplace. These groups each have different perspectives on the role of the pharmacist in the modern healthcare system. Far too many pharmacists overlook the professional service opportunities that exist outside of direct patient care. Each stakeholder group has a unique role in the healthcare system, and value strategy trained pharmacists can expand the universe of their business options by designing professional services custom tailored to the targeted needs of a stakeholder.

See page 106 for a graphic depiction of the stakeholders.

Tier One Stakeholders

The tier one stakeholders are the patients, their extended families, and the unpaid caregivers who provide help with daily activities such as meal preparation, transportation, bathing, shopping, child care and medication administration. Their primary focus is on providing a better quality of life for the patient.

Tier Two Stakeholders

The tier two stakeholders are the professional caregivers trained to legally diagnose and/or treat disease or provide wellness services. This group includes doctors, pharmacists, nurses, physician's assistants, nurse practitioners, licensed caregivers, dentists, podiatrists, physical therapists, and any other health professional that provides direct patient care. This tier seeks value not only for their patients, but also for their business operations. Because their business model is to treat or prevent patient illness, a portion of their value strategy is aligned with the outcomes for their patients but goes beyond patient care to include the profitability of their professional practice and their compliance regulations.

Tier Three Stakeholders

The tier three stakeholders include the employers, insurers, governmental agencies and taxpayers who ultimately decide which bills get paid. The interests of these stakeholders logically include all of the economic, clinical and humanistic outcomes of the tier one and tier two stakeholders, but their interest expands to include the provision of population based care. Tier three stakeholders typically focus less on individual patient treatment and more on managing the overall costs of providing care to a large group of patients. Sometimes a patient's therapeutic goals may not perfectly aligned with the payer's budget. Payers must be concerned with utilization rates, the cost-effectiveness of outcomes, fairness and not overspending on one patient at the expense of others.

Tier Four Stakeholders

The tier four stakeholders include the governmental agencies that regulate health care. Regulators write, revise, and enforce rules, and regulations governing the practice of health care and the licensing of health professionals. These stakeholders typically focus on preventing fraud, waste, and abuse more so than scrutinizing the quality of care for individual patients. Their role in the health care marketplace is more about protecting the public interest than optimizing patient care. This creates a conflict for individual patients when their interests take back seat to the interests of the needs of public policy.

Tier Five Stakeholders

The tier five stakeholders are ancillary providers of goods and services to any of the other stakeholders. This tier includes software developers, legal services, marketing companies, research teams, drug wholesalers, drug and device manufacturers, office equipment suppliers, payroll services, raw materials suppliers, and many others that add value to the overall group of healthcare stakeholders. This is one segment of the healthcare industry that has not traditionally been considered members of the healthcare team. Yet these stakeholders affect the cost, quality, and productivity of healthcare delivery. Software tools, diagnostic equipment, on site lab analysis, patient care web portals, and everything from the people that clean the building to people that research new therapies impact the provision of high quality care.

I know this might seem a little too academic for some of you but let me explain why this is so important. There are many ways to use your pharmacy training to benefit society. Direct patient care is only one of the options. Many pharmacists have been lost to follow up over the years because they are no longer practicing in a traditional role. And yet these individuals used their training as pharmacists to start software companies, become lawyers, to enter politics as an elected official, become corporate officers of large organizations, developed data management companies or some other valuable enterprise.

Again while we purport to be an evidenced based profession we are failing to systematically review all of the evidence to justify selecting pharmacy as a career choice. There are so many really interesting things that people are doing after having received their pharmacy degree that are simply off the radar for most people decided which profession to enter. This hurts the profession in my opinion, because we are narrowly defining our value in only one stakeholder arena, that of direct patient care.

The reality is that some of us directly impact patient lives by being directly involved in their care and others of us create our value by indirectly impacting their care through serving clients within Tiers 2 through 5. The truth is that if the profession does not expand it's definition of value we risk having that value narrowly defined by others.

Remember that the goals for tier four regulators is less about optimizing care than protecting the public from fraud, waste and abusive over-billing. If we want to optimize patient care those best practices must be defined and refined by care providers not regulators. The points of view are incongruous so without effective provider input the results of top down regulatory policy are likely to not be very good.

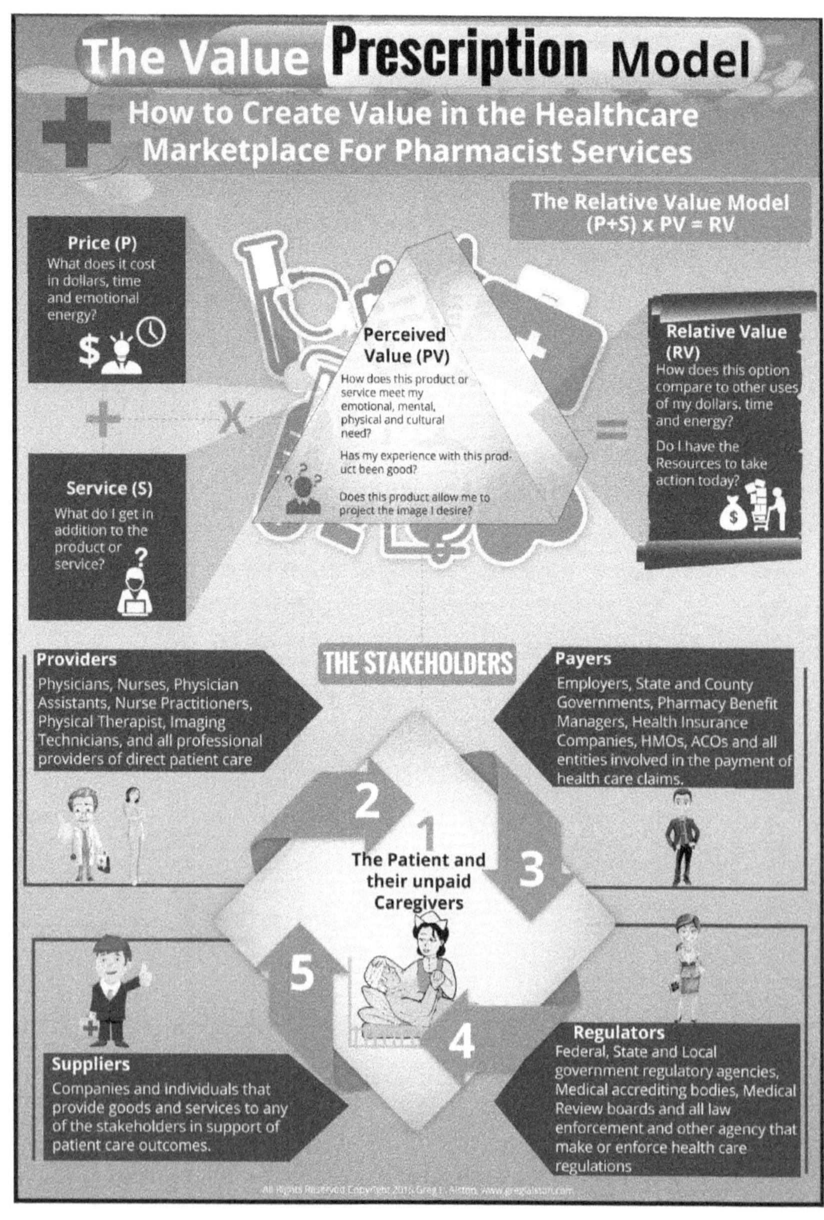
The Value Prescription Model
How to Create Value in the Healthcare Marketplace For Pharmacist Services
The Relative Value Model
(P+S) x PV = RV
Price (P)
What does it cost in dollars, time and emotional energy?
$
+
X
=
Service (S)
What do I get in addition to the product or service?
Perceived Value (PV)
How does this product or service meet my emotional, mental, physical and cultural need?
Has my experience with this product been good?
Does this product allow me to project the image I desire?
Relative Value (RV)
How does this option compare to other uses of my dollars, time and energy?
Do I have the Resources to take action today?
THE STAKEHOLDERS
Providers
Physicians, Nurses, Physician Assistants, Nurse Practitioners, Physical Therapist, Imaging Technicians, and all professional providers of direct patient care
Payers
Employers, State and County Governments, Pharmacy Benefit Managers, Health Insurance Companies, HMOs, ACOs and all entities involved in the payment of health care claims.
1
The Patient and their unpaid Caregivers
2
3
4
5
Suppliers
Companies and individuals that provide goods and services to any of the stakeholders in support of patient care outcomes.
Regulators
Federal, State and Local government regulatory agencies, Medical accrediting bodies, Medical Review boards and all law enforcement and other agency that make or enforce health care regulations

CHAPTER 10

The 17 Steps in the Value Strategy Formula

The process for creating a value strategy is relatively simple. The effort required to do it correctly is not. Greg L. Alston

There are three big initiatives that I believe the profession has been dead wrong about. I don't think anybody has been doing this intentionally to harm the profession and yet I think the lack of progress the profession has made primarily emanates from some of these misguided assumptions.

1. The Field of Dreams Strategy

As I said earlier, one mantra that has been pounding through the profession for the last 40 years is what I call the field of dreams strategy. We have felt that if we build it, they will come. We have believed that if we improved the clinical skills of our professional pharmacists that the public would willingly pay for these new services. However, this has failed to happen, and it has failed to happen because leadership misunderstands how value is created for a target market.

A February 2018 article in the *American Journal of the Pharmacy Association,* MTM Economics 101: Supply vs Demand, pointed this out very clearly when their survey of patients who had been exposed to medication therapy management services came back with some unexpectedly negative results. Approximately 60% of the patients who were aware of the services and aware of what the pharmacist could do, said they had no interest, or very little interest in receiving the services.

Let me tell you what I think this means. It does not mean that those services are not valuable. It does not mean that people don't need those services. What it means is our profession has done a terrible job of marketing those services. We argue with ourselves. We write articles in our journals. We complained to our legislators. But we have never made a compelling case to our patients (or other stakeholders) that what we do is critical for their health.

There is no more clear proof of this than comparing what pharmacists have done for their profession to what dentists have done for their profession. If you ask any adult in America how often they need to go to their dentist to have a good thorough cleaning and inspection they will tell you every six months. If you ask anyone in America how often should a person taking multiple medications go to their pharmacist for a complete medication review, you will be met with blank stares. Again, we have done a mediocre job of marketing our profession.

One of the unintended consequences of focusing most of our time and energy on improving clinical skills for new graduates has been the diminished focus and interest in the business side of the profession. The majority of students graduate with clinical aspirations but with no idea how to make a living with their clinical skills. Pharmacists are afraid to market their services and ask to get paid. They are afraid to start their own businesses or develop new business models. They have a singular outdated version of how pharmacists create value in the marketplace. They are focused on dollars per hour instead of value.

Another unintended consequence of focusing so heavily on clinical skill development has been a negative impact on job satisfaction. The fact that a large number of working pharmacists do not practice in an environment that allows them to fully utilize their clinical skills in their daily work is disheartening for many. This has led to increased dissatisfaction with the job after graduation. And this dissatisfaction in the ranks has spilled over into discouraging young people from entering the profession. Ten years ago, only 2-3 % of pharmacy students reported wishing they had chosen a different career on their graduating student surveys. Now this number has increased to over 10% of graduates. And that is before any of them have really entered the workforce. As of the year 2018, the profession is having difficulty attracting enough qualified applicants to fill all the seats in the schools of pharmacy. The total number of applicants is shrinking.

2. Technology Will Set You Free Strategy

Another misguided assumption that has been percolating for years is the idea that technology will set the pharmacists free to do their job better. The huge mistake here has been that leaders have failed to differentiate between sustaining innovations and disruptive innovations. The technologies they tout as wonderful have largely been sustaining innovations like robotic dispensing devices, automated Pyxis machines, automated packaging devices, technicians, central fill and computerized messaging services. All of these sustaining innovations have one simple goal to reduce the amount of pharmacist labor needed to fill a prescription.

As a result, many employers have used these technological innovations as a way to reduce payroll and not expand services. Translation: less pharmacists needed. And here is the brutal reality of this issue. It is not the employers job to guarantee any employee that they will never lose their job. It is their duty to provide value to their stakeholders. If you don't want to lose your job then you need to become an integral part of the value solution for your organization or you have no honest argument for continued employment..

Your duty to the employer, your customers and your family is to give a full effort everyday to further the mission of customer value. However, while working for any large organization you are always at the mercy of cutbacks, or loss of business or market conditions that force changes over which you have no control. You can lose you job despite having done a good job. Therefore, you must always dedicate a portion of your workweek to improving your skill sets and increasing your capacity to create valuable service because you never know when you are going to need to re-engineer your career.

The real power of technology will be when disruptive innovations create entirely new markets in which pharmacists can operate and charge for their true value. Failing to differentiate between sustaining and disruptive innovations has caused confusion and led to misguided action. We need to stop repeating the misconceptions and start living the truth. Those of you with great ideas need to create technological innovations that improve patient outcomes and when that happens patients will gratefully pay for what we do. But you must liberate your brain from the dollar per our mindset in order to see the possibilities.

3. Health Systems Pharmacy Practice is the Future of Pharmacy

And another unhelpful mantra that pharmacy leaders, especially in the academic realm, have been touting is that health systems clinical practice is the one true path to being a good pharmacist. The drive to require everyone to do residencies and to advance their clinical skills to become better pharmacists however is also a bit misguided in the context of the modern healthcare marketplace.

The facts are that over 60% of all pharmacists practice in the community pharmacy setting and it is likely that over 90% of all patient encounters occur in the community setting. In addition, Medicare policy drives hospital policy. Medicare is likely to be insolvent in the next few years. The government is essentially predicting that Medicare will be unable to meet its obligations soon. What this means is that health care systems payment policies are now geared to keeping people out of the hospitals. Hospitals are rewarded for shorter stays. Hospitals are penalized for readmissions. Less than 25% of all pharmacists work in health systems positions and according to the Bureau of Labor Statistics that percentage is not predicted to change much over the next few decades. So how can the future of pharmacy practice be in health systems pharmacy practice that only employs less than one third of pharmacists?

Again, this does not mean that what health systems pharmacists do is not valuable. The extremely talented pharmacists working in those environments do awesome work. But they will likely never be more than 33% of working pharmacists if you believe the projections of the United States Department of Labor. Plus they are getting paid less than community pharmacists in many cases. And they will never perform the number of patient encounters that the community practice pharmacists do. According to Beckers Hospital Review , dated 2-18-15, about 15% of Americans are classified as patients on any given day meaning that 85% are not.

The big challenges we have in medication adherence, compliance with therapy, transitions of care, and achievement of patient outcomes all need to be managed in the community environment. That is where people live. That is where they have access to the pharmacist. And that is where those services can be paid for. New hospitals are simply not being built. Small hospitals are being absorbed into big hospitals. Large hospital systems are consolidating their clinical services to centralized formats. This means that it is highly likely that less pharmacists will be working in that environment over the near future.

Why is this important for you to understand? If you wish to have a long and prosperous career in the practice of pharmacy you are going to have to learn how to create valuable services for paying customers, how to market those services effectively, and how to sustain that value over the length of your career.

What this means is that your Doctor of Pharmacy degree can get you a job, but it is your business skills that are going to determine your financial success. If you believe that your employer is going to look out for you and your family, then you are essentially abdicating responsibility for your family's future. And, in my opinion, you are taking a huge risk with your future financial health.

Some important questions to ponder

Ask yourself honestly, if your employer is sold in the next few years are you going to financially benefit from that transaction?

Are any of the activities that you are performing today things that can be outsourced or down-shifted to a less expensive employee?

Are you willing to trust that your employer will guarantee you a job for the rest of your life?

Are you ready to choose yourself as the captain of your fate?

Are you aware of what can you do about it?

1. Find a market niche that you are interested in being an authority for.
2. Identify the pain in that marketplace
3. Craft a solution to solve that problem
4. Start a business that will allow you to earn income in that niche
5. Perfect the niche and grow the business to become a full-time replacement income.
6. If you are uncomfortable starting a business then be smart enough to partner with an innovator as a member of her team.

Where would you rather be five years from now? Still working and doing what you're doing? Or in charge of your own fate in producing your own income? There is no right or wrong answer to this question. Not everybody wants to be in charge of their own destiny. I understand that. But there are 10 to 15% of you that secretly yearn to run your own business. If you're ready to take steps to make that happen then you need to start making progress towards that goal.

Launching your own new business can be exciting but also a bit frightening if you have never done it before. The good news is that anyone can learn to build a value strategy that works by following a sound value strategy development process.

The way to guarantee your progress towards success is to break a large task down into manageable bites. What follows is the 17 steps for turning your idea into an income stream. The end game is to develop a value strategy to become the best in the world at what you do. I call this the ***Value Strategy Formula.***

1. *Identify the Niche*

Select a niche that is big enough to make a living and small enough to dominate. Pick a topic, disease state, area of interest, or healthcare problem in which you would like to become an authority. There are many ways to become an authority and there are many spins on each potential target area. You can provide service to patients, to other providers to payers to regulators or to any of the other stakeholder groups. What area are you most interested in?

2. *Create an Avatar for your Niche*

An Avatar is a composite representation of the hopes, dreams, fears and goals for your target market customer. Describe your Avatar using a target market insights chart, name the Avatar and select an image as a visual representation of your Avatar. In this stage you are attempting to complete a psycho-graphic and demographic profile of your target customer.

So what does your Avatar dream about, fear, or long for? What problem is she trying to solve? What words does she use? What pain has she described?

3. *SWOT the Niche*

Once you've chosen a niche you need to spend some time reflecting on the strengths, opportunities, weaknesses and threats that exist in that marketplace. Then begin thinking about how to capitalize on these with your own unique plan. It is crucial you understand what your competition does well and where they have weaknesses. Ideally you want to find a strategy that your competitors can't or won't respond to.

4. *Scope the Practice*

Your new business enterprise cannot do all things for all people especially at the beginning. At this stage you should describe the scope of your practice in its first iteration. The goal is to get a minimally viable product launched and then learn from your launch to improve the business.

5. *Craft a Plan to Improve Outcomes*

What is your plan to improve the intended outcomes for your Avatar? The goal of creating any business is to solve problems for your avatar. If your business plan does not solve the pain in the marketplace for your Avatar, it will never succeed. What problem do you hope to solve? How will you solve it?

6. *Align your Personal and Business Values*

One of the biggest mistakes rookie entrepreneurs make is they chase money and profits rather than pursuing a passionate area of interest. If your personal values and your business values are not aligned, you will get bored with the business over time and fail to give it the energy and enthusiasm it needs to succeed. Does your idea align with your personal value structure?

7. *Strategize transformational value for your market*

This is truly the core of your business strategy. If what you do does not create transformational value for your Avatar, then you will be wasting your time. Transformational value means taking somebody from where they are, and don't want to be, to where they want to be. How will your business idea transform your Avatar?

8. *Develop a marketing strategy*

Describe the key elements of your marketing strategy. How do you plan to attract new leads and convert them to paying customers? There's a big difference between marketing strategy and tactics. Radio ads are a tactic. Google ads are a tactic. Can you outline an effective marketing strategy based on value theory? Do you have a sales message or are you building an educational no-sell selling system?

9. *Craft a compelling strategic marketing statement*

Write a 125-word or less statement that describes the value strategy in terms that your Avatar will find compelling. Your goal when you are done is that your Avatar should say to herself, "I would be crazy not to buy this?" Planning tactics before crafting a strategy is a fool's errand.

10. *Make an Irresistible Offer*

Your offer must be believable. It must have a high return on investment for your Avatar and be wrapped in your core values. It must make your prospect think. "I would be flippin crazy not to use your service."

11. *Brand Your Authority*

What is your Brand Purpose? What will be your Brand Differentiators? What will be your Brand Personality? What will be your brand strategy? How will you build your authority as an expert in this niche?

12. What will be your monetization strategy?

How will you get paid for your strategy? Will you generate a digital product, book, blog, pod cast, video channel, e-learning course, telemedicine practice, consulting practice, I-Tribe practice, or some other idea?

13. How can you use technology to go location free?

How can you take advantage of technology to break the money for time barrier? Can you use Webinars, Cell phone Apps, Conference software, Facetime, Encrypted email, VOIP phone etc to create a location free business model?

14. What is your customer care strategy?

What processes and tools will you use to provide expert customer care? How will you guarantee your customer who has issues gets those issues resolved quickly and effectively? Great ideas with poor execution will fail.

15. Explore Joint Venture Strategies

Can you work with other people to share access to customers? Who else serves your client with a non-competing product? Can you develop an affiliate network program?

16. Craft an Action Plan

List the things you must do to turn your plan in to reality. Prioritize your list and add due dates and reminders.

17. What Can You Do to Move Your Project Forward Today?

Take a few minutes of uninterrupted time each day to set your action items for the day. Select something everyday that moves your project forward. Never skip more than one day without doing something to move your idea forward. Even one small step is better than leaving the idea unattended.

The relative value theorem describes the buyer decision making progress which is necessary to understand how buyers come to perceive something as worth spending their money on.

Relative Value = (Price+Service) x Perceived Value

The process for designing a valuable business model includes:

1. Identifying a pain in the marketplace,
2. Crafting a solution to ease that pain, and
3. Crafting an offer to be put in front of people that is a clear win for them.

And the process for creating an income generating sustainable business model from your big idea is the 17 step Value Strategy Formula I just outlined. The last chapter will focus on an innovative idea called the I-Tribe practice model that uses all of these techniques to propose an innovative model that could revolutionize the practice of pharmacy.

If you would like more information and/or training about how to create your own income producing value strategy then contact me at: http://greglalston.com/contact-2/ and we'll chat.

CHAPTER 11

The I-Tribe Practice Model

In 2013 I authored an article for the *Journal of the American Pharmacist Association* with a colleague, Jenn Waitzman. The article described the I-Tribe Community Pharmacy Practice Model concept as a futuristic practice idea. The synopsis of this article read:

"Modern pharmacists could provide a disruptive innovation in the marketplace for primary care by taking advantage of new technology and implementing the I-Tribe Community Pharmacy Practice Model (I-Tribe). This innovation would provide new primary patient care services directly to patients in a cost-effective and profitable manner that could be implemented without third-party payers acting as intermediaries, while simultaneously providing a new source of revenue for community practice pharmacists. The key elements to disrupting the market for professional primary care services would be positioning a new pharmacist-based service at the low end of the market and targeting the service to satisfy simple needs that existing providers have no interest in or inclination to providing."

The analysis stated: "Community pharmacy practice has experienced multiple sustaining innovations that have improved dispensing productivity but have not stimulated sufficient demand for pharmacy services to disrupt the marketplace and provide new opportunities for pharmacists. I-Tribe pharmacy could be the disruptive innovation that expands employment opportunity for pharmacists, insulating them from the types of sustaining innovations designed to reduce the costs of providing care and eliminate the need for dispensing pharmacists.

Entrepreneurial innovation through I-Tribe pharmacy would free the pharmacist to become the care provider envisioned by the profession's thought leaders."

Is Innovation Good?

Most people misunderstand the concept of innovation. Not all innovation is good for employees. Most innovations are 'sustaining innovations' such as electronic medical records, computerized claims management, robotic dispensing devices, Pyxis machines, automated inventory reorder systems and the like. These sustaining innovations are designed to decrease the amount of payroll required to do the job. The net effect of a sustaining innovation is usually less people doing the same job. It does not move the practice forward in a new direction that increases access to a new audience. It simply makes the existing practice paradigm more efficient.

When people speak glowingly of innovation, they typically mean 'disruptive innovation.' Disruptive innovations are those innovations that create new opportunities and expand the number and variety of opportunities. A disruptive innovation is one that challenges the existing practice paradigm and opens up never before dreamed of opportunities. Something perceived to have no value can suddenly skyrocket to a position of great value in the wake of a disruptive innovation.

Let me give you a quick example. Two hundred years ago land in rural Texas that was too dry for farming was considered to have very little value. Then the automobile was invented. And these automobiles needed gasoline. And someone discovered that some of that arid, unproductive land provided easy access to underground supplies of crude oil. All of a sudden, the land became very valuable because it produced a million barrels of oil per year. The disruptive innovation of replacing the horse with a horseless carriage created entirely new industries and reshaped the value of previously worthless assets.

Something like Amazon.com is a disruptive innovation that has led to changing the way people shop for goods and services. This has had a huge impact on the viability of malls and big-box stores. In addition, it has provided thousands of entrepreneurs with the ability to make money using the Amazon.com platform. But lots of department store employees are now out of work.

Another example of a disruptive innovation was the development of Netflix. This video delivery service essentially made the video rental store obsolete. Does anyone remember Blockbuster video stores? Where are they now? While this innovation disrupted the video store industry it actually led to the development of new streaming video services. Disruptive innovations make old technologies or business models obsolete, but they also create fantastic opportunities for people who understand how to take advantage of the innovation.

Think for a minute about the way that we deliver healthcare in this country. You get in your car. You drive to the doctor's office. You wait in the waiting room until you finally get in to see the doctor. The doctor spends 3-4 minutes with you and either writes you a prescription, sends you for more tests or tells you, " you're fine." If you go to a general practitioner and you have a lung problem they send you to a pulmonary specialist. If you have a kidney problem they send you to the urologist. If you have a skin problem they send you to the dermatologist. At the end of the day you may see several different doctors and still no one has taken it upon themselves to make sure they have solved your medical problem.

You may not understand this when you are young and haven't had to go to the doctor very often. But I can tell you as a person on the other side of 60-years-old that it is very difficult to find an actual doctor who will stop and take care of whatever it is that ails you. Each doctor visit costs money, time and aggravation. In any case, you have to pay for the visit and take time off from work to go to all these different appointments.

When you think about it, this business model has not really changed for a hundred years. Yes, there are computers and fancy diagnostic machines, but patient care delivery is 1-to-1 and you spend very little time with the actual person who knows what they are doing.

If a doctor writes a prescription it is sent to a pharmacy. The pharmacy dispenses the medication directly to the you. The pharmacist spends a minute or two with the you before sending you home. Essentially what this means is that after a you have spent 3 to 4 hours at the doctor's office (and perhaps visited more than one doctor's office), and at least an hour or so to get your prescription filled, you still haven't received much in the way of patient-centered healthcare. During this 5 to 6-hour adventure you have spent no more than 5-10 minutes with the MD and PharmD responsible for your health.

Is it really any wonder that the utilization of medications in this country is so messed up? Remember, at the beginning of this book I told you that the NCPA report in 2013 estimated medication problems cost this country almost $300 billion per year. It is probably much worse than that in indirect costs.

There has been a lot of attention paid to such things as medication reconciliation but there is no system for actually doing it well. Patients are released every day from the hospital with a long list of medications that may or may not look anything like the medications they were taking when they entered the hospital. Most processes are internal to the hospital and they never communicate directly with the community pharmacist.

I can tell you from my experience at Best Pharmacy in Sun City that hospital formularies rarely match community practice formularies. Therefore, many seniors end up doing one of two things: 1) taking both sets of medications or 2) taking neither. The medications they were prescribed by the hospital never match the ones prescribed by their primary care physician. Obviously, this causes severe problems. The patients are either under-medicated or over-medicated.

What if we created a new disruptive innovation? What if any patient that wanted to could spend 30-60 minutes with a highly trained medical professional that could actually solve their problems? What if they could do that without ever leaving the comfort of their home? What if you could take all the things that you say over and over to each new patient and have your patients watch you say those things on a video rather than in person? What if your patients could spend an hour with you on video without you spending more than 5 actual minutes with them? And what if you could expand your patient base to include any patient in the world. How cool would that be? That is the promise of the I-Tribe practice model.

For this I-Tribe practice model to work as a disruptive innovation, pharmacists will need a new tool to provide primary patient care services directly to patients in a cost-effective and profitable manner. They will need to be able to do this without the interference of third-party payers. The keys to launching this disruptive innovation for professional primary care services will be:

1. Positioning the new service at the low end of the pricing market.

2. Targeting the service to satisfy simple needs that existing providers have no interest in or inclination to provide.

This will establish a marketing beachhead for strategic growth in to more sophisticated services in the future. I know that it is not only possible it is relatively easy to do. I believe the technology platform to make it happen will be available soon.

I would recommend that all of you read an awesome book by Seth Godin called, *Tribes: We Need You to Lead Us.* In his book Seth describes the tribe; "the tribe is any group of people large or small who are connected to one another through a leader and an idea." He explains how the intersection of Internet and software technology has made the creation, funding, nurturing, and growth of Online tribes possible. The Internet has eliminated the major barriers to geography, cost, and time that previously made forming a tribe large enough to make a living very difficult.

The success of any tribe will depend on the leader of the tribe. If the tribe members are passionate about the idea around which the tribe is centered, a passionate leader can digitally engage this tribe and become quite successful. The I-Tribe practice of pharmacy will thrive when an engaged pharmacist tribal leader identifies a focused topic around which a group of patients will organize, understands the key issues that the group wishes to have solved, develops a transformational solution for their problems and delivers that solution in a way that is beneficial to tribe.

The I-Tribe members could come together in an interactive virtual community that will allow for the education of the tribe, communication with the tribe leader as the professional mentor, and create 24 hour a day, seven days a week, 365 days a year access to an energetic group of engaged tribe members willing to help each other. A properly constructed interactive web presence is feasible today with inexpensive technology well within the reach of any pharmacist.

All that is needed for the pharmacist is a well-constructed web presence, an Internet marketing strategy, and the suite of communication tools to make effective communicating with the tribe manageable. The missing ingredient is not the technology but the enthusiastic enlightened pharmacist willing to build their own I-Tribe practice.

Done correctly, the tribe members will pay the tribe leader with credit cards or Pay Pal accounts that make fiscal intermediaries like PBMs and insurance companies unnecessary. If the I-Tribe leader can construct a proper value strategy they will be able to attract patient or client payments.

And here is where the synergy of community practice and ambulatory care specialists could reign. Every pharmacy has a computer full of customer data. This data could be mined to identify diabetic patients, asthma patients, patients with anxiety or any other subset of patients. The pharmacy owner generalist could then offer products and services to these patients and share in the revenue while enhancing the quality of care. Now that would be disruptive innovation!

The Process for Creating an I-Tribe

Step 1-Identify the niche

You must identify a niche market that is large enough to support the business plan and willing to spend money on the service but also be small enough where you can become a recognized authority. Disruptive innovations always begin at the low end of the market in price. This brings an entirely new audience into the process. Designing your new patient care service will require that you consider three major issues. If the answer to all three of these questions is 'Yes" you may have found a great innovation model:

1. Does the innovation target customers who have been unable to do it for themselves in the past due to lack of money or lack of skill?

2. Are people seeking answers to basic healthcare questions and is your innovation aimed at customers who would welcome a simple product?

3. Will the innovation help customers do for themselves more easily and effectively those things they are already trying to do?

Step 2-Develop A Sound Business Plan

After identifying a good target market niche, you can test whether that business model could result in a disruptive innovation by seeking answers to these two test questions.

Are the existing products in the market more than good enough for the target market's needs?

Do healthcare consumers have a reliable source of accurate peer-reviewed information that is targeted to their comprehension level?

In essence, you are trying to discover whether the existing healthcare system meets the information needs of the modern Internet savvy healthcare consumer. Information is abundant and cheap. Anyone can look up anything on the Internet. Some sites report good quality information and other sites are simply sales letters. Can your typical customer tell the difference? Will they make terrible health care decisions based on some bogus information that they find on the Internet? For example, can a Hollywood celebrity talk them out of getting their children vaccinated?

There are really three types of healthcare consumers out in the market today. There are **highly informed** consumers that read good information and know more about their disease than many medical practitioners. These people are considered highly informed.

There are also many people who are **highly misinformed.** They have read sketchy Internet information and believe it to be true. And third, there are people who are so overwhelmed by the volume and difficulty of the information they read that they simply refuse to consider it all and therefore become **highly confused.**

The I-Tribe leader must be able to detect the information state of the people in the tribe and provide the appropriate learning for the information state of their tribe member.

Step 3-Make An Irresistible Offer

Irresistible offers are a very special kind of sales offer made in a very special kind of way. Properly targeted to your tribe these sales offers are compelling and explain exactly what you do and how you do it. The key components of an irresistible offer are that your offer must include:1) a high return on investment for the buyer, 2) a touchstone theme that is clear, simple, short and immediately understood as a central tenet of the tribe; and 3) it must be believable.

Again, Internet marketing technology makes the delivery of this message well within the budget of any new entrepreneur.

Step 4: Lead the Tribe

For the I-Tribe to thrive, the leader must be a passionate advocate for the tribe's main goals and the leader's vision must resonate with every member of the tribe. The leader must understand the vision of the tribe, why the tribe exists and communicate often enough to be helpful but not so often that it's considered annoying. Everyone is sick of having their name on a list where someone sends them an email every day trying to sell them something. That would be a great way to turn off your tribe.

Your communication must be honest, sincere, forthright and true. The only way you will succeed in creating a strong professional reputation with your tribe is to earn it every single day. The way you create a competitive advantage that attracts your tribe members to you and your tribe is to choose a niche that capitalizes on your expertise, your communication skills, and your talent for problem-solving within this focused niche. Many pharmacists will not be capable of operating a successful I-Tribe practice model. And even those who are capable will require additional training in the creation of a value strategy and learning the techniques to build and maintain a tribe.

Nevertheless, every pharmacist could benefit from the expansion of opportunities created by these I-Tribe entrepreneurs if the affiliate business model can be used to share the revenue created by tribe activities with referral sources of targeted leads. This is precisely why I believe that the community care practice generalists can learn to generate additional income, at the same time they are maximizing the value to their patient, by partnering with I-Tribe practice pharmacists to offer enhanced services to their patients.

Do you really believe that patients will pay in order to receive information Online directly from pharmacists? The answer is an undeniable yes. If you don't believe me go to Clickbank.com and look at the hundreds of products on healthcare topics being sold to consumers every day in this country. When you do so, the first thing you'll notice is that none of these products are written by pharmacists. All of these products would be more successful if they were delivered by knowledgeable pharmacists.

Here is the Secret to Success

Let's say that you want to earn $120,000 a year as a pharmacist running your I-Tribe. The normal pharmacist tries to find one employer to pay them $120,000 a year or whatever the going salary is. That strategy has worked for quite some time. An I-Tribe pharmacist can use an entirely different metric. You could earn the same income using a variety of pricing models. You could have 120 people paying you $1000 per year. You could have 240 people paying you $500 per year. You can have 480 people paying a $250 per year. Or you could have 120,000 people paying you one dollar per year. In all these instances you would earn the same amount of money.

The beauty of the I-Tribe model is that you can use them all. You could have an entry-level product that was delivered entirely Online for just a few dollars. You could have a higher priced product that includes a monthly consultation for a few hundred dollars. And you could have a full-fledged consulting model that would cost a few thousand dollars.

The opportunity is there. Are you willing to put in the time and effort to learn how to do it? Or are you going to be still whining five years from now that you're not really practicing the way you want to practice?

One way that pharmacy entrepreneurs can start their first business is with an information product because they are relatively inexpensive to develop and launch.

The beauty of this kind of educational product is that once you create the content you can make it accessible to hundreds of people at the same time without requiring you to be Online with them. If your materials are well constructed and provide great value to your tribe you can charge reasonable fees and reserve your private time for consultations with those that require more focused attention.

By being able to offer an entry-level product at a low price you can potentially make powerful, life-changing, clinical information for patients available at an extremely really low price. Hence you have the opportunity to create a disruptive innovation. And here is the secret sauce in the I-Tribe model.

This low-cost product educates clients to trust and rely on your information so that when they are ready to purchase more expensive assistance they will call you and be prepared to spend what is required to get the job done. Your opening price point product essentially becomes your lead funnel to your higher priced consultation products. Again, any pharmacists can learn to do this you just need to get the proper training and you must be willing to develop your expertise as an I-Tribe leader.

For any business to be successful, it must attract interested potential buyers and these are called 'leads'. Those leads must be converted into first time buyers. First-time buyers who receive great value for their purchase will become engaged customers. Engaged customers will be willing to spend more with you to get advanced coaching and consultation.

The secrets to success are to generate targeted leads, convert those leads into sales, get your first-time customers to buy additional products, and then learn to develop additional revenue sources that make those customers highly profitable. That is the business flow for any business.

The professional flow for this business is to identify problems that a target niche is having in the marketplace, figure out solutions for those problems, figure out how to deliver that solution effectively in a highly scalable manner, and then establish yourself as the world's best practitioner in your specialty. Essentially you need to become the world's best I-Tribe leader for your tribe.

And here's the one last thought to ponder. Some people are really good at being entrepreneurial but historically this has been less than 15% of pharmacists. Many pharmacists are much better at the process and practice of patient care than innovating new business models. Typically, a patient care oriented pharmacist is not all that excited about starting their own business. Which leads me directly to the point that many of the thought leaders in our profession have just flat out got wrong.

We don't need more clinical training and credentialing to move the profession forward. In actuality, many pharmacists are not working in a place where they get to maximize the use of that training.

If you really want to push the profession forward, we need to get our entrepreneurial pharmacists to start more businesses that can capitalize on the clinical training of our patient-care oriented pharmacists.

READ THIS LAST PARAGRAPH AGAIN!

One good entrepreneur could end up hiring 20 or 30 pharmacists to run the clinical side of their business. One good entrepreneurial pharmacist could start a network that will integrate the access to patients available in community practice with the clinical training of our ambulatory care specialists.

As I said at the beginning of this book, we need to stop arguing about which of us uses our PharmD better and start demonstrating our value to the marketplace by building disruptively innovative business models that prove to our stakeholders that we can do things for them that other health professionals either can't or won't.

I call on all of you to eliminate and reject the long-held biases of "clinical" versus "community" and come together to embed high-end clinical services within the businesses of innovative, generalist, community practice pharmacists to improve the quality of the healthcare system in this country. Community practice is, was, and always has been the entry level primary care provider for the entire healthcare system.

Group-think pharmacists who are waiting for us to be listed as federal providers are doing you no favors by suggesting that you can't offer services without that status. Every day in America people are buying inferior healthcare from grocery store shelves, websites, infomercials and magazine ads. It has personally made me crazy over the years that people will walk into a vitamin store and spend hundreds of dollars on some product recommended by an 18-year-old muscle head when that product may actually be harmful and ruin their kidneys. (Whey protein in high doses for example.)

Find your niche, develop your expertise, build out your business model, and change the world one patient at a time. Waiting for permission is a prescription for failure. Waiting for provider status is an excuse for inaction. Waiting for evidenced-based practices to prove that your business model is sound is absurd. Entrepreneurs succeed because they try something and see if it works.

Quotable Thought

The only way for pharmacists to show real value to our communities is to start delivering value to those we serve.

Here is your charge. Communicate with your customer audience. Illuminate their problems, concerns and unsolved issues. Find a way to solve those issues for them. Build the business model to make that happen. Then make them an irresistible offer to provide that service. You don't need permission, you simply need to take action.

Once you achieve your success please get in touch because I would like to share your success on my website. Only when pharmacists see other pharmacists being successful will they realize that they too can break free of the artificial barriers to professional practice. Barriers that are keeping them from fully appreciating the incredible impact they can have on their patients.

Yes, it is absolutely stupid that dietitians are officially healthcare providers and pharmacists are not. It is crazy that physician assistants and nurse practitioners have less training on medications than we do yet they have prescriptive authority and we have to get their permission to make a necessary medication changes for our patients. But that's the way it is. We complain about our status as providers and we allow people outside the profession to determine the scope of our practice and the computation of our value.

We need to stop whining amongst ourselves and take our case straight to the people who love us the most, the American public.

Remember this, the public has voted that pharmacists were one of the most trusted professions in the country for as long as the poll has been taken. It used to flop back and forth between us and nurses as number 1 and 2. And when the public is answering this survey, the pharmacist they have in mind is the community practice pharmacist. Not the academic, not the researcher, not the internal medicine clinician but the person they see in the pharmacy they use.

There has been a bad trend in ratings over the past 6 years. We are now below nurses, military officers, grade school teachers, and medical doctors when we used to be ahead of them all. I believe a big part of this decline is the self-inflicted wounds we have administered on our profession by failing to unite around a common purpose. We have allowed large multi-site employers to devalue the profession by under staffing their stores and damaging the reputation of our front-line community pharmacists. We have aired our dirty laundry in public and dramatically decreased the number of college students interested in the profession. We have allowed our profession to be defined and commoditized by PBMs and discount card operators. We have failed to communicate our real value.

For example, PBMs and insurance companies have conspired to shift prescription dispensing into mail-order prescription mills under the false assumption that these dispensing mills reduce the cost of medicine. This is not likely to be true. If you don't believe me go to the NCPA website to review all of the fraud, waste and abuse of seniors they have uncovered. Senior citizens have hundreds of bottles of unused medications stuffed into drawers all over their houses because they can't turn off the flow of drugs from mail order dispensing factories. Therefore, our most frail patients, with the highest number of chronic diseases, who must manage the most complicated drug regimens, are being mailed bags and bags of drugs and being expected to figure out how and when to take them. Simple logic would tell you this is a bad idea.

An entrepreneur will figure out a way to solve this problem. A primary cause of senior hospital admissions is medication misadventures. Medication misadventures are also responsible for a great percentage of patient falls and broken hips. If you care about health care in this country, then stop tolerating this pitiful charade of sick care being foisted on the citizens of our country and start providing truly valuable patient care services.

Whereas a community pharmacy must maintain temperature control for every drug in their possession we allow mail-order pharmacies to jam stuff into a bag and leave it in mailboxes that can reach 160° temperatures. The USP guidelines on the appropriate temperature control during the mail shipping of drugs is frequently abused by shippers and the practice goes on unchecked.

Yet when one bad actor pharmacy violates regulations, as in the case of New England compounding pharmacy debacle, immediate massive regulations that undermine the very nature of pharmacy practice acts are rushed into service by our regulators. Pharmacists were the original compounder of medications and now are largely prevented from providing customized medication solutions for our patients without onerous regulations and expenses.

Hey y'all when there was a shortage of pharmacists we took advantage of that market by getting raises and bonuses because the employers needed us to keep stores open. Now with a surplus of pharmacists we need to take a different approach.

One Final Thought

I would like to leave you with one final thought. Think about your dentist for a moment. How often are you supposed to return to the dentist for a checkup and a teeth cleaning? Everyone in America knows you're supposed to go to the dentist every six months.

The typical senior citizen in the United States has at least three chronic diseases, seven drugs in their daily drug regimen, sees multiple physicians and gets their medications from multiple pharmacies. Ask any one of them how often they should go to their pharmacist for a complete medication review. (CMR)

I will guarantee you that none of them know the answer. Do pharmacists even agree on the answer?

Why do they not know how often they need to see their pharmacist?

Who is responsible for getting them to know that?

I am sorry y'all, but we are failing in our duty to this nation. It is high time we stopped using excuses and start delivering value to those we serve. If we don't provide value to others then we should not expect to get paid for what we do.

Creating value for others, marketing that value and sustaining that value over time is the prescription for success. The future of pharmacy lies in independence from the self-limiting beliefs of our past and complete devotion to the principle of:

TThe Key to Success is to Create Value for Those You Serve. Your Wealth Flows Directly from the Value You Create for Others.

There are five types of stakeholders that can be served. Don't limit yourself strictly to patient care. If you want to learn how to create value for your stakeholders then get value trained.

Price, service and perceived value, are the key to creating value in the marketplace for pharmacy services.

You can get some free value training by subscribing to my blog and following my posts at www.greglalston.com. I will do everything I can to help you succeed. And send me your questions and I will get them answered for you.

It is impossible to put everything you need to know in a book because the process I recommend to create a value strategy has several steps and the trajectory of each step depends upon the conclusions you make on the previous step. So as in all projects the devil is in the details.

Here is to your financial independence,

The Value Strategy Guy.

Given the rapidly changing marketplace for healthcare I want to remind you of the sage advice, **"He who hesitates is lost"** There is debate about who said it first but the truth is timeless and extremely relevant to today.

Can you afford to wait?

Check out www.greglalston.com to discover the latest tools, tips and recommendations to help you achieve success.

In general, to form your personal consulting practice you will need the following tools.

- A website that clarifies the niche for your intended audience
- A secure platform to deliver password protected content.
- A e-mail auto-responder service
- A lead funnel process to get prospects on to your e-mail list.
- A marketing research and content strategy to attract people to your tribe.
- And a tool for scheduling your appointments and communicating with your clients.
- And the time an energy to put it all together.

"The Value of an Idea lies in the Using of it." Thomas Edison

"The best way to find yourself is to lose yourself in the service of others" Mahatma Gandhi

"The real measure of your wealth is how much you'd be worth if you lost all your money." Unknown

"A wise person should have money in their head, but not in their heart."Jonathan Swift

Afterword

Author, Educator, Pharmacist, Entrepreneur, Speaker

Our Creed

The Key to Success is to Create Value for Those You Serve. Your Wealth Flows Directly from the Value You Create for Others.

We believe that community-based practice is the past and future of the profession. We believe that community pharmacies are the most frequent providers of primary healthcare in the country. We believe that the greatest opportunities to create financial freedom for your family over the next 20 years will be in developing services for the non-hospitalized patient. And we welcome ***all*** of our clinical brothers and sisters to join us in the community because that is where people live. And that is where they can be best served.

My personal value strategy is:

To help frustrated, overworked professionals worried about the state of their profession, select and implement the best value strategy possible so they can get paid what they are worth and build a secure future for themselves and their families.

I have an enjoyed a long, interesting career in community practice pharmacy and education. After starting out as an educator, I became a chain drug guy, then an independent store owner, then returned to academia to teach pharmacy students. Along the way I started a chain of Halloween Shops, a medical billing company, an Internet-based lead generation business, and a property management firm. I also served for three years on the Board of Directors of Independent Pharmacy Coop in Madison Wisconsin and several other volunteer boards including the Menifee Valley Hospital Foundation Board, the Pharmacist Recovery Network, and the Matthews Free Medical Clinic.

By far the most rewarding and successful business I have ever owned has been the Community Drug Store. There is just something special about having a positive impact on people's lives and practicing pharmacy in the old fashioned, high service, high value mode. Real people love real pharmacists that provide real care. And community care, not acute care, provides more patient encounters per week than any medical provider. Therefore community practice has the greatest potential impact on our nation's health.

My Personal Mission is:

To instill the will to be great, the desire to excel, and the ability to create value, in the next generation of pharmacists.

I believe:

We all have a "God Given" skill that makes us unique and personal faults that make us human. Our challenge is to find the uniqueness in each other and overlook the faults.

I have many faults, but my singular unique talent is the ability to observe things that others don't see yet and to integrate those observations into effective action. This manifests in my being a voracious reader and collector of seemingly unrelated information that becomes the foundation for breakthrough ideas. I have been tested by a variety of instruments and rate in the 99.9th percentile on creative problem solving.

There are four primary modes of problem solving. Most people are wired to be one of four types. After testing over 500 pharmacists for their type, I have found that 15% are Creative which means they find creative solutions to problems. About 15% are Implementers which means they don't come up with the idea, but they are good at implementing ideas within an organization. About 30% are Refiners which means they analyze your decisions and uncover why your solution won't work. And about 40% are Executors which means they are best at taking the plan and turning it in to action. They are the worker bees that get stuff done. Pharmacists, in general, tend to be more process driven and better at working and refining processes than the general population, but they tend to be less creative in solving problems.

If you are looking for a solution to energize your career, then I hope that this book has helped provide you with some options. I would love the opportunity to help you to create value for the stakeholders you serve by helping you learn the skills you need to compete in the new economic climate of healthcare reform.

Random Thoughts to Ponder regarding the destructive power of pessimism.

"Positive self talk is important in determining who you will become. Be careful not to let the pessimism of others derail your opportunity to succeed." Greg L. Alston

"There is a real danger of unintended consequences, of encouraging people to give up. Pessimism, if it becomes a habit, can reinforce a narrative of unstoppable decline. If there is nothing we can do, that releases us from our obligations." David Grinspoon

Read more at: https://www.brainyquote.com/quotes/david_grinspoon_913794

"Pessimism never won any battle." Dwight D. Eisenhower

Read more at: https://www.brainyquote.com/quotes/dwight_d_eisenhower_149110

"Pessimism leads to weakness, optimism to power." William James

Read more at: https://www.brainyquote.com/quotes/william_james_378646

Although the original source of this quote is difficult to identify the wisdom of the passage is not.

Watch your thoughts, they become your words;
Watch your words, they become your actions;
Watch your actions, they become your habits;
Watch your habits, they become your character;
Watch your character, for it becomes your destiny

Optimism on the other hand has a strong relationship to high performance and success

Optimism is the faith that leads to achievement. Nothing can be done without hope and confidence. Helen Keller

Perpetual optimism is a force multiplier. Colin Powell

Optimism is an expectation that good things are going to be plentiful. The wealthy generally have the sense that life will bring good rather than bad outcomes. That doesn't mean they believe that good things will be omnipresent, but that they will outnumber the not-so-good. Jean Chatzky

Sharot, T. (2011). The optimism bias. Current biology, 21(23), R941-R945.
Hansen, M. D. (2003). Optimism breeds success. Professional safety, 48(5), 8.
Fredrickson, B. L., & Joiner, T. (2002). Positive emotions trigger upward spirals toward emotional well-being. Psychological science, 13(2), 172-175.
Crane, F. G., & Crane, E. C. (2007). Dispositional optimism and entrepreneurial success. The Psychologist-Manager Journal, 10(1), 13-25.
Lyubomirsky, S., King, L., & Diener, E. (2005). The benefits of frequent positive affect: Does happiness lead to success?. Psychological bulletin, 131(6), 803.
Shepperd, J. A., Maroto, J. J., & Pbert, L. A. (1996). Dispositional optimism as a predictor of health changes among cardiac patients. Journal of research in personality, 30(4), 517-534.

Other Books by Greg L. Alston

The Bosshole Effect: Three Simple Steps Anyone Can Follow to Become a Great Boss and Lead A Successful Team.

How to become the boss that your employees would willingly pay to work for instead of the person who sucks the life, energy and enthusiasm out of their day.

Available in Paperback and Kindle editions on Amazon.com.

Ten Things a New Manager Must Get Right from the Start

What to do when you get promoted to help you be successful in your first management job. Especially designed for pharmacists who just got promoted to their first management role.

Available in Paperback and Kindle editions on Amazon.com.

Pharmacy Management: Essentials for All Practice Settings
McGraw-Hill Textbook Editions 3, 4 and 5

Available wherever McGraw Hill Textbooks are sold.

Co-editor of the compilation and chapter author for
Chapters on: Creating and Managing Value, Operations Management, and Risk Management.

Resources Available to Help You Develop Your Own Value Strategy and begin charting Your Own Future

A Free introductory video course in which I explain How to Create, Market and Sustain Value from a pharmacist's perspective can be accessed at:

www.pharmacistsuccessacademy.com

You can download a free 17 step guide to creating a value strategy at: www.greglalston.com

If you would like contact me about speaking at your event or anything else you can find me at: www.linkedin.com/in/greglalston

References on Value Strategy:

Alston, Greg L., and Joseph C. Blizzard. "The value prescription: Relative value theorem as a call to action." Research in Social and Administrative Pharmacy 8.4 (2012): 338-348.

Zgarrick, D. P., Alston, G. L., Moczygemba, L. R., & Desselle, S. P. (2016). Pharmacy Management: Essentials for All Practice Settings, 4e. Chapter 3: Creating and Managing Value

Alston, G. L., & Waitzman, J. A. (2013). The I-Tribe Community Pharmacy Practice Model: professional pharmacy unshackled. Journal of the American Pharmacists Association, 53(2), 163-171.

How to contact the VIP Pharmacists and organizations mentioned in the body of this book.

Dan Benamoz and Pharmacy Development Service can be found at: https://www.pharmacyowners.com

Dr. Blair Thielemier and the Pharmapreneur Academy can be found at: https://pharmapreneuracademy.com/ref/12/

Dr. Anna Garrett and Rev Up Your Midlife Mojo can be found at: http://www.drannagarrett.com/

Dr. Michelle Fritsch and Meds Mash can be found at: http://www.medsmash.com

Dr. Patti Manolakis of PMM Consulting LLC can be found at: https://www.linkedin.com/in/patti-manolakis-a587a714/

Dr. Sue Paul of SyneRxgy Consulting can be found at: http://www.synerxgy.com/

Dr. Matt Johnson of Amplicare can be found at: https://www.linkedin.com/in/johnsonmatthewh/ and also at: https://amplicare.com/

CPESN: Community Pharmacy Enhanced Services Network https://cpesn.com/

The Pharmacist's Letter: https://pharmacist.therapeuticresearch.com/Home/PL

"You can only become truly accomplished at something you love. Don't make money your goal. Instead, pursue the things you love doing, and then do them so well that people can't take their eyes off you."
Maya Angelou

"If money is your hope for independence you will never have it. The only real security that a man will have in this world is a reserve of knowledge, experience, and ability."
Henry Ford

www.ingramcontent.com/pod-product-compliance
Lightning Source LLC
Chambersburg PA
CBHW020206200326
41521CB00005BA/264

9781632970169